In Spirit and Truth

United Methodist Worship for the Emerging Church

In Spirit and Truth

United Methodist Worship for the Emerging Church

L. Edward Phillips and
Sara Webb Phillips

OSL PUBLICATIONS
Maryville Tennessee

In Spirit and Truth
United Methodist Worship for the Emerging Church
(revised edition)

Copyright 2006 by L. Edward Phillips and Sara Webb Phillips
second printing July 2008
This book is printed on acid-free paper that meets
the American National Standards Institute Z39.48 Standard

Produced and manufactured in the United States of America by
OSL PUBLICATIONS
P O Box 5506
Maryville TN 37802
www. Saint-Luke.org

Cover art by Don Drumm. Used by permission
www.dondrummstudios.com

ISBN 978-1-878009-53-1

Scripture quotations, unless otherwise indicated, are from the New Revised Standard Version of the Bible, copyright 1989 by the Division of Christian Education of the National Council of the Churches of Christ in the USA. All rights reserved. Used by permission.

The Order of Saint Luke is a religious order dedicated to sacramental and liturgical scholarship, education and practice. The purpose of the publishing ministry is to put into the hands of students and practitioners resources which have theological, historical, ecumenical and practical integrity.

www.Saint-Luke.org

Contents

Acknowledgments 7

An Invitation.. 9

One   Worship in the Real World 14

Two   Worship in Spirit and Truth 33

Three   With All the Company of Heaven 49

Four   Finish, Then, Thy New Creation 68

Select Bibliography 91

Acknowledgments

Books on Christian worship arise from the communities that have nurtured the authors. We are grateful for the various communities with which we have worshipped over the years, and also for the colleagues whose support has encouraged and often challenged us.

Our United Methodist friends from the Memphis Annual Conference have continued to love and admonish us on various issues of worship and discipleship, even though we have not lived in that part of the world for most of our ministry. Among the many other pastors, teachers, and musicians who have offered support, we would like to thank Dean Francis, Steve Long, Ron Anderson, K. K. Yeo, Jerry Jelsema, and Vera Lynn and Randy Sheets. We especially want to thank the lay members of our churches, among them Conrad Damien, Ed de Rossett, Dan Howell, David Koehler, and Bonny Roth.

Finally, we want to thank OSL Publications for issuing a second edition of this book, one that takes into account the passing of the General Conference study of Holy Communion, *This Holy Mystery.*

Truly God is good, all the time!

Edward and Sara Webb Phillips
March, 2006

An Invitation from the Authors

Renew your church, Lord, your people in this land.
Save us from cheap words and self-deception in your service.
In the power of your Spirit transform us,
and shape us by your cross. Amen.[1]

David Letterman's "The Late Show," has a recurring comedy bit called "Is This Anything?" During the bit, a screen rises to reveal a novelty act in progress on stage. After viewing the act for a few seconds Letterman and Paul Schaffer (the band leader) give their immediate opinion whether what they have just witnessed at that moment is, in fact, "anything."

We love this wonderful bit of post-modern humor. And, incidentally, we think that this is precisely the question that faces many contemporary Christians gathered for worship. Someone leads a prayer, and the voice in our head asks: "Is this anything? Are we really speaking to God? Is God listening? How would we know?" The congregation joins in a song of praise: "Are we addressing the God of Creation"? We say a thanksgiving over bread and wine and call them what they obviously are not—the body and blood of Jesus—and wonder, "What *is* this, anyway?" Or, as some often put it—is this "just a ritual"? "Merely a symbol?" In short, "Is this anything?"

Yet, despite the skepticism many of us bring to church, we continue to hope that Christians long for worship that is "something" genuine and profound, because we believe that Christian life and identity are rooted in, shaped by, empowered for mission through the worship of the church. On the other hand, we also think that the decline of mainline Protestantism within the last half of this past century is significantly related to worship that does not seem to be about anything of consequence, worship that does not challenge and does not transform.

We are overwhelmed with all the research and writing about the dying church, and with the projections and prescriptions to renew the church. It is distressing to experience "worship wars" between denominations and within local churches. The discussion of what makes for "right" worship has led us to debate what is really at the heart of being Christian. Is worship about being baptized and partaking of the Lord's Supper? Is it serving those who suffer? Is it giving praise and thanks to God? Is it all of these and more?

We have read about the shift in paradigms of worship and in church life in general. The call for renewal, even redesign, in the hope of finding renewed authenticity in the church has come through loud and clear. Church growth, evangelism and worship resources now abound. While almost every suggestion has truth behind it and some of the resources can provide a helpful corrective to inauthentic patterns of church life and worship, something has not clicked for us. Something seems to be missing from attempts to renew worship through uncritically employing the means and methods of the culture around us, while mostly abandoning historic, ancient, or even biblical patterns of prayer and praise. In part, what we miss is the recognition that ritual is fundamental to our faith and life; for we are creatures that need basic patterns. We also miss the recognition that our rituals connect the church's identity across congregational and denominational lines to God's vision for the world; through our comprehensive practice of worship, we embody God's New Creation. In faithful, authentic, Christian worship we receive our identity as the Body of Christ.

Or, at least, that is the way it is *supposed* to work. Today, however, United Methodists are in an identity crisis, which is most obviously manifest in our public worship. On any given Sunday we find among United Methodist congregations such a variety of liturgies and styles that we might wonder what, if "anything," these churches hold in common. We seem to have lost much awareness of how we as United Methodists connect from congregation to congregation, much less to the universal Body of Christ. While many of the changes we have experienced in recent years may have been for the good, we believe that the time for experimentation is over. Now we must find out how to reconnect to the United Methodist liturgy (which Methodists have traditionally called "The Ritual") which is biblically grounded, theologically sound, and contextually relevant, but which also connects us to the liturgy of the universal church — on earth and in heaven. The renewed understanding of worship proposed here is that United Methodists must claim and *authentically practice* our liturgy to allow it to shape our identity and ministry for the twenty-first century.

What we offer into the already expansive body of writing on the church's worship is, hopefully, a fresh look at the scriptural and historical background that many congregations already know, and a fresh link to the dynamic tradition and ritual of the church all congregations already possess. In other words, United Methodists already have at their disposal incredible resources to bring the Gospel to contemporary culture. We recognize the work of those who are developing creative and sophisticated methods to attract people to the Christian faith. The late twentieth century saw a renewed interest in the "experience" of worship, with congregations employing all sorts of novel methods and technologies to "enhance" the worship experience of church-goers. Technologically-skilled production, toe-tapping music and well-constructed "messages" can stir the more complacent. The emerging church of the twenty-first century, however, is asking the post-modern question of their experiences — "Is this anything?" What Christians need is not merely a good "experience," but an experience *of something,*

something authentic, something with substance that is deeper than the fleeting moment. Which is to say, we are longing for an experience of some-*one*, the living presence of our Lord. We believe that the Wesleyan heritage and the church's ancient, biblical patterns, when faithfully employed, will be *better* able to captivate and motivate future generations of Christian seekers and Christian disciples.

When the first edition of this book was published in 2000, little had been written about worship in the emerging church. Six years later, the Emerging Church Movement (it has a name now!), with its re-appropriation of historic liturgy, sensual ritual and catholic sensibility has gained considerable momentum. The particular trends we identified six years ago are stronger now, and we believe the need for attention to the problems we identify is even more urgent.

Chapter one examines the cultural, theological and religious assumptions that guide our contemporary North American society; how we are losing our belief in a sure foundation for the truth in religion or culture. How do these current assumptions affect how the church thinks of itself (its identity) and its practice (its ministry)? How do these assumptions affect how the church thinks about worship and how it organizes itself for that ministry? Chapter two uses five scriptural models to understand the meaning and purpose of the church at worship. How do these models present worship as an alternative worldview? Chapter three addresses the tradition. How do the early church, the early Methodists, and the movements of the more recent past provide insight into the meaning and practice of worship in the present? Chapter four proposes an approach to worship that connects local congregations to the universal church through the United Methodist Ritual. We will present some practical guidelines for United Methodist churches to consider as we prepare for the coming decades of the new millennium.

When our youngest daughter was three years old, we would often hear her singing songs of the popular *Veggie Tales* video series. After watching a couple of tapes a few times, she knew several of the songs by heart. When frightened at night, she would sing "God is bigger than the Boogey Man." And, when she was looking for something, we would could hear her singing "Where is my hairbrush?"

Good liturgy can also become imprinted on our imaginations like that. "The risen Christ is with us!" "Free us for joyful obedience!" "In the name of Jesus Christ you are forgiven. Glory to God!" "Let us give thanks to the Lord our God!" "Holy, holy, holy Lord...Heaven and earth are full of your glory!" "We give you thanks for this holy mystery in which you have given yourself to us; grant that we may go into the world in the strength of your Spirit to give ourselves for others." Imagine what a community immersed in such authentically Christian prayer and praise might become! We know the answer: the Body of Christ in the world. May the reflections within these pages stimulate your thinking toward that end.

ENDNOTES

[1] "For Renewal of the Church", from South Africa, *The United Methodist Hymnal* (Nashville: The United Methodist Publishing House, 1989) 574. Henceforth we will abbreviate its reference to *UMH*.

Chapter One

Worship in the Real World

From the cowardice that dares not face new truth,
from the laziness that is contented with half-truth,
from the arrogance that thinks it knows all truth,
Good Lord, deliver me. Amen.[1]

Occasionally, someone in our churches may be heard to say, "Why can't the church today be more like the church in the good old days?" This question implies that if we contemporary Christians would only be like our more faithful forebears, we would not have the sorts of problems we face in our churches today.

What was the church like in those "good old days"? The Apostle Paul in his letters gives us a picture of life in the "good old days" of the New Testament church. In many cases, he writes his letters because the churches are having problems: sexual immorality, spiritual immaturity, strife between the rich and the poor, and theological disputes. The church in Corinth was even having major difficulties with the celebration of the Lord's Supper (1 Corinthians 11) and with how to construct a good order of worship for their meetings (1 Corinthians 14). If we move ahead seventeen centuries to the early Methodist revival, we find that John Wesley had to deal with similar problems: doctrinal disputes over predestination and grace, political disputes about the American Revolution, community disputes over the recognition of women preachers, and the list could go on.

Here is the point: we *are* like the church in the "good old days." Just as Paul, and John Wesley, and any number of other important figures in our Christian history found it necessary to call the church to renewal, we too find ourselves facing a need for renewal. Indeed, the church will be in a constant process of renewal until God brings history to its conclusion. Until then some dissatisfaction with the church will be the *status quo*. Renewal is not something we will do until we accomplish our goals; renewal is the ongoing process of seeking to be ever more faithful to the call of Jesus, the longing for a deeper experience of holiness before our Holy God. Therefore, if we find ourselves dissatisfied with some aspects of our worship, we may be on the right track!

On the other hand, we are unlike the good old days in that our culture is experiencing a communication revolution (more accurately, explosion) unknown in any other time of history. This new age of technology has begun to reshape the way we get daily information, the way we pay for groceries, how we turn on our lights (if we even do it manually anymore) and certainly, for Christians, how we experience and understand worship. Fast-paced music, colorful environments, and soundbyte sermons are attracting the first generation to be raised with daily access to a computer, cell phones, and cable television. These challenges bring exciting and difficult times for the worship life of the church.

WHAT IS WORSHIP SUPPOSED TO DO?

Congregations express their dissatisfaction with worship in many ways. Generally, we might group the concerns into two very different camps: those who advocate traditional worship practices, and those who seek to promote more contemporary, popular worship practices. Most will agree however, that something needs to change in the way we worship.

A great deal of change has already been taking place in our worship practices over the last forty or so years. In the closing decades of the twentieth century, we have seen dramatic revision in the worship books of many of our churches. Roman Catholics, Episcopalians, Lutherans, United Methodists, and several other denominations have revised their "official" liturgies and hymnals. This has created tension within some churches, as change usually does. Many older church members especially have found themselves longing for the old liturgies with familiar "church" language. Yet, the newer worship books are grounded in historical liturgical patterns of the church. The language which the newer worship books use may sound more like contemporary English, and the hymnal may include many contemporary hymns and songs, but, overall, these newer books are still very much in continuity with the traditional liturgies of the church.

Some Christians have found these liturgical books to be inadequate to meet the particular demands of the times because, their use of more contemporary language notwithstanding, they seem to be more connected to the past than to the present world. Timothy Wright, to cite one critic, describes several "drawbacks" to traditional or liturgical worship. To begin with, Wright claims liturgical worship is confusing to those who are unfamiliar with the official worship books and their idiosyncratic organization. Moreover, these books use "religious language" that is unrelated to the lives of many who come. He asserts traditional worship often involves music that is difficult to sing and in a classical style that is not very popular with people today. Furthermore, according to Wright, liturgical worship emphasizes awe and reverence for God to a degree that can hinder personal intimacy among the people.[2] To overcome these barriers, Wright advocates a "contemporary" model of worship used by many growing congregations that is especially designed for those who have not grown up in church. The contemporary model views worshipers as "consumers" who value innovation, immediate gratification, a variety of choices, high performance quality, personal experience, the feeling of intimacy, informality, and accessible popular music.[3] Wright and other advocates of the contemporary worship style argue that worship must be exciting in the same way that a good movie or rock concert is exciting, or those who come once probably will not come back. According to this view, in order to communicate the Gospel to our present age, we must package it in a form that makes it attractive and usable. As Wright argues, we must not confuse the style of worship (which is totally arbitrary for every setting) with the substance of faith (which is the eternal truth of the Gospel).[4]

The debate between advocates of "traditional worship" and "contemporary worship" rages in many of our congregations, among our laity and clergy, and in the pages of our denominational magazines. Many have not noticed that "traditional worship" and "contemporary worship" operate with very different understandings of what worship *is supposed to do*. Traditional worship emphasizes stability in order to ground the congregation in the eternal God: stately worship for the Rock of Ages. Contemporary worship emphasizes entertainment to entice seekers to Christ: friendly, upbeat worship for the Gentle Jesus.

Each of the approaches has validity; each has its limitations. We want to suggest, however, a more basic purpose for worship: faithful worship is the way God forms us through the story of Jesus Christ by the power of the Holy Spirit in the practice of living according to the Truth. *Worship begins in what God does in us.*

WORSHIP IN A POST-MODERN WORLD

In worship, therefore, God forms us in living according to the truth. What we mean by "truth" is seeing the world the way it really is: that is, from God's point of view. We might assume that this should be fairly obvious. The world is all around us; we have but to observe it. But, of course, things are not quite that simple. First, mere observations can never offer us all the facts that might tell us what the world is like. Most of us have never "seen" an atom, yet we believe atoms exist. Second, all of us have preconceptions of "the way things are" which may mislead us. The notion that the earth was the center of the universe (there were many "facts" which supported this idea) prohibited many intelligent people in Europe from being able to accept the validity of the observations of Copernicus and Galileo.

This second difficulty has been particularly problematic for modern science. Therefore, the period in Western European history that we call the Enlightenment broke the hold that tradition held over scientific investigation and belief.[5] We may legitimately learn from past authorities, but we must always be willing to make a critical evaluation of the authorities based on new observations through new experiments. In this view, the past is merely one, and by no means a privileged, source of understanding.

The basic assumption of the Enlightenment, and the modern world that it spawned, is that if we were only clear-headed enough, we would all see the world in the same way. This notion was applied not just to natural science, but also to social science, ethics, and even to religion. Religion especially proved to be a problem because there are so many religions in the world. Worship proved to be an even bigger problem because it appeared to be even less objective and more diverse. Nevertheless, the assumption of the modern-enlightenment view of the world is that from a purely objective perspective there could be only one true religion. This assumption could lead to very different conclusions regarding Christianity. One could determine that Christianity, as it is grounded in the Bible and its foundational doctrines, is the one religion (if it is properly understood) that is objectively and verifiably true. That is, Christianity is essentially a set of factual propositions which are verifiable the way all facts are verifiable. All other religions are, at best, wrong to the degree that they diverge from Christianity. Indeed, from this perspective, Christianity (and especially its book, the Bible) is objectively true even as it touches upon science or history, since there cannot be contradictory "truths." In this approach, however, worship tends to become rather austere since worship is not easily reduced to a set of propositions.

The other, more modest, approach would be to understand Christianity as one approximation of some universal religion, which all religions approximate to some degree. The differences in beliefs and practices are merely diverse expressions of the deeper truth of God. The more we seek common ground with other religions, the closer we will understand the universal experience of God to which they all point. From this position worship is very arbitrary since it is merely a way to express religious feelings or experiences of God which transcends all specific religious, cultural, or personal beliefs and practices.

What the second approach has in common with the first approach is the assumption that there are foundations of truth *independent of a particular historical tradition and authority* which one could use to verify the reality of religious belief or worship practices.[6] This is an attractive notion: if religious belief is a true view of God (or the world), then it ought to be available generally to everyone in the world. This is both democratic (we all have equal access to the truth) and fair (no one is privileged).

The problem is that there are no people in general; we all live in particular communities with particular traditions, including our religious traditions. While there is common ground between some of the "world" religions (for example, belief in One God is shared by Jews and Muslims), most religions have distinctive beliefs and practices that they cannot abandon without giving up what is essential to that religion (for example, to discount the resurrection is to render Christianity pointless). By seeking to get beyond the particular religious beliefs of the various religious traditions we might be able to construct an idea of God (or Ultimate Realty, since not all religions have a belief in a god) that, in theory, anyone could believe in, but no one actually would. In short, the whole Enlightenment project, which has defined the modern world, has slowly been abandoned with the recognition that there is an irreducible diversity to our understanding of God or of Ultimate Reality. We are beginning to realize that the Enlightenment notion that we need to escape our particular traditions in order to understand the truth is itself a particular tradition of belief *that is not shared by most people outside of the Western European intellectual tradition.*[7]

With the breakdown of the modern worldview of the Enlightenment, we have begun to enter a period that many philosophers and theologians call "post-modern." In our "post-modern" world the modern understanding of Ultimate Truth is called into question, but not in order to replace it with a more adequate "Ultimate Truth." Rather, claims to truth are often seen as ways to establish power over others, to manipulate them for cynical ends. This cynical view of truth is given by a teen-aged girl named in Lily Tomlin's one-woman show written by Jane Wagner, *The Search for Signs of Intelligent Life in the Universe.* Agnus, who is estranged from her scientist father comments, "The last really deep conversation I had with my dad was between our T-shirts. His said 'Science Is Truth Found Out.' Mine said, 'The Truth Can Be Made Up If You Know How.'"[8]

One contemporary way we approach the manipulation of truth is through escapism, or, as it is now known in the computer world, "virtual reality." The manipulation of reality affects what we eat (sugar-free desserts and fake-fat chips), what we listen to (orchestrated music produced by synthesizers), what we watch (highly realistic violence), and where we vacation (Disney World's virtual Europe rather than a trip to Germany). This is nothing new of course; some churches have had plastic flowers on their altars for years. Any of these examples are not necessarily bad – but they are not real. An addiction to "virtual truth" can dull our ability to engage the real world.

How can we avoid cynicism or escapism if there are no universally verifiable foundations for truth? We might give up all attempts to interact with those outside of our tradition and withdraw into our own cultural or religious subculture. Or we might look for a way that is open to interaction with other traditions, cultures, and worldviews, while acknowledging that we come from a particular tradition that leads us to ask certain kinds of questions and propose particular sorts of answers to the questions we receive. We might see our own particular religious tradition as our gift from God which we offer to the world with a mixture of boldness and humility as witnesses to what God has done among us. That is to say, we could become like the blind man in John 9 who admitted he could not answer all the questions that the religious leaders put to him about Jesus, but nonetheless testified, "One thing I do know, that though I was blind, now I see" (Verse 25b).

If Christians cannot claim verification for our testimony to the truth apart from our own particular tradition, neither can anyone else. We are all in the same philosophical swamp! However, this is not cause for despair, but rather for renewed vigor in our churches. We Christians are quickly finding ourselves in a world in which we can be witnesses to the truth of Jesus Christ, free of the delusion that this ought to be common sense, or that it is possible to see the truth of Christianity without conversion. We have a story to tell that presents a coherent understanding of God and our world; it may not be the only viable story that human beings tell about God's relationship to the world, but it is a story that we know from our own experience to be true. In a world that has lost its belief in a coherent story, this will be good news.

Let us return, now, to the debate between "traditional" and "contemporary" worship. We suggested earlier that these two approaches to worship are based on different assumptions about what worship is supposed to do. They also suggest very different reactions to the problems of the emerging post-modern world. Those in our churches who advocate "traditional" worship want to hold on to a way of being Christian that offers continuity and stability in a changing world. For some people in our churches, this means looking back to an era when Christians could act as if theirs were the only viable way of being religious - a time when stores closed on Sunday, and First Church on the Corner was the only place where "good people" were expected to be. The most characteristic aspect of this view of worship is not its use of "liturgical" hymns or language or printed orders of worship, but its nostalgia for an age when mainline Christian denominations were dominant in American culture. As our religious climate has become more pluralistic, this clinging to "tradition" can become little more than a sentimental longing for the past. On the other hand, those who advocate "contemporary" worship have assumed that pluralism has produced a "buyer's market." If the church is to have a marketable product, then we have to make a pitch for the widest possible range of ever changing personal tastes with all the enthusiasm of the most exciting and manipulative television commercial. Yet worship that is as transitory as the latest advertising gimmick cannot avoid appearing to be another throwaway item. Indeed, in our self-centered materialism and hunger for entertainment we are in danger of "amusing ourselves to death."[9] This is the sort of cynicism and escapism we should want our worship to be able to challenge.[10]

Neither of these approaches will serve the church well in our emerging post-modern world. *What we need is a way to worship that grounds us in tradition without sentimentality and inspires enthusiasm without self-centeredness.* As we suggest above, we need a practice of worship that forms us through the story of Jesus Christ by the power of the Holy Spirit in the practice of living according to the Truth.

WORSHIP AND THE STORY OF JESUS CHRIST IN HISTORY

While we may typically use the word "tradition" to talk about the historical continuity of a religion, we might better think of this as "story." Our story, the Christian story is grounded in the biblical narrative but goes beyond it to include the lives of faithful women and men who have joined their lives to the story of the Bible until the present. It is a story of great faith and (let us be honest) of horrible failings. However, it is a story which, overall, testifies to the power of God in Christ to free us from sin and free us for joyful service in the world.

Our Christian story has a master plot that operates on several levels. First there is the catholic story, "catholic" meaning "universal." We affirm this whenever we say the Apostles' Creed at a baptism or confirmation: "We believe in the holy catholic church..." In a real sense, the affirmations found in the Apostles' Creed form an essential part of this catholic story that we share with all Christians throughout the world. The Apostles' Creed is a short, summary version of the Bible, which is itself an essential source of the story. From the catholic story we also receive many of our liturgical practices, such as baptism and the Lord's supper, preaching the Word of God, our basic understanding of those who lead worship and sacrament in the ministry (both lay and ordained), and our worship of the Trinity. This story is catholic because almost all Christians throughout history have shared it, although we might disagree on how to interpret or practice this point or that. This story is also catholic since it allows us to see the church as connecting all the diverse cultures and ethnic groups which make up the church in the world. We know we are worshiping as Christians when we find ourselves participating in this universal story of the church in all times and places.

The Christian story comes to us, however, in a particular way through our more recent traditions. Those of us who are United Methodist received the catholic story through the ministry of the early Methodists, German Evangelicals, and United Brethren. From the work of John Wesley and others, we received a story of a religion of the heart, that we may know God with assurance by the witness of the Spirit within. We received a story that leads us to strive for social holiness along with personal holiness as we seek the faith that leads to Christian Perfection.[11] From Charles Wesley, we received the story in song, as he was the hymn writer of the early Methodists. Our United Methodist story includes a commitment to being a connectional church, with each congregation tied to other congregations in our work of ministry. The simple fact that we have a *United Methodist Hymnal* demonstrates our connection with other United Methodist congregations. Furthermore, we received the understanding of the Christian life as a discipline that we must undertake; indeed, the quintessential United Methodist book is called the *Discipline*. We know we are worshiping as United Methodist Christians when our worship contains the themes and the identifying words and practices of this story.

But, of course, we live the catholic story and the United Methodist story within our own local congregations. Our congregations have their own narratives, which are as diverse as the number of congregations that exist. This story is made up of baptisms and funerals, weddings and confirmations, religious revivals and angry disputes. It is the story of new buildings and new mission outreach programs, wise elder saints and brash young seminarians, Sunday School teachers and choir directors. The congregation will also have a particular cultural setting that will include the ethnic traditions within that culture. Congregations will have favorite hymns and distinctive ways of celebrating the Lord's Supper, traditions of Easter Sunrise Service and Christmas Eve pageants. We know we are part of the story of our congregation when we find ourselves sharing in the problems and blessings of living with our brothers and sisters in the weekly worship of the local church.

There is one final subplot in our Christian story, and that is our personal story. This is the story of how faith has been awakened within us, whether we came into the church as an infant or have come as an adult, and how we live out our own prayer and praise, not only in relation to our local congregation, but within the other communities that lay claim to us: family, work, neighborhoods, civic organizations, and so forth. We know we are a Christian personally when we find the call to Jesus Christ coming to us in our daily lives as we interact with all the various communities in which we find ourselves.

There are, then, four basic levels of the Christian story: catholic (universal), United Methodist (denominational), local (congregational), and individual (personal). When we see harmony among these various levels, our Christian identity is clear and our worship is authentic. When individual Christians find a meaningful place of worship in their local congregations, and when these congregations demonstrate the character of the universal church, then we have an authentic and integrated Christian identity in our worship. Our life as a Christian makes sense to us and we know who we are in relationship to the world.

WORSHIP: EMBODYING THE STORY OF JESUS CHRIST

In our worship, God forms us in a way of living in the world, and this way is the story of Jesus Christ. Christian faith is more than assent to a set of propositions, and it is more than having certain feelings of religious experience. Indeed, it is more than knowing or even believing in a certain story, if by this we mean a mental or psychological acknowledgment. Advocates of "contemporary" worship suggest that the central ideas of the gospel are all that is important, and that the style or actual practices of worship are totally arbitrary as long as we get the ideas across to our congregations. Some of us might wonder that if having the right ideas about God is all that is important, then why bother with worship at all? However, worship *is essential for Christians if we want to move beyond believing with our heads to believing with our hearts.* To be even more graphic, authentic Christian faith requires that we believe it in our *guts.* It must be an *embodied* belief.

If worship involves our bodies, and not just our thoughts, it is best that we think of worship as a set of actions or practices as well as ideas. We will examine three dimensions of the practice of worship: worship as ritual, worship as word, and worship as worldview.

WORSHIP AS RITUAL

Rituals are patterns of behavior that express the beliefs and values of a community. While it is possible to have private rituals (for example, brushing one's teeth before bedtime), even private rituals indicate the beliefs and values of a community (we probably learned to brush from our childhood family). Ritual behaviors can be as complex and culture-specific as table manners or as simple as a handshake greeting. But each ritual encodes within our bodies our understanding of what it means to be a part of a community, to share in its system of beliefs. When we stand to hear the scriptures read, bow our heads to pray, or touch the hand of a fellow worshiper in a sign of peace, we are practicing the fundamentals of our faith with our bodies. French sociologist Pierre Bourdieu suggests that ritual practices express our most deeply held beliefs, even those that defy clear verbal explanation.[12] This "irrational" aspect of ritual—that it occurs without a great deal of mental reasoning—has caused ritual to be very suspect in the modern world. Indeed, Sigmund Freud and his followers believed that rituals are little more than immature ways of handling our conflicts with reality.[13] For Freud, community rituals are a sort of group-sanctioned neurotic compulsion.

Most of us who find ourselves in church Sunday after Sunday would not agree with this Freudian theory of ritual. Still, many of us are suspicious of it. "That's just a ritual!" is a common way of describing something in worship done out of habit, rather than out of conviction. Those of us who are Protestant Christians want to have clear reasons for our worship practices so that we can do them with conviction. We need to do more than practice rituals with our bodies; we want to be able to believe them with our minds. Indeed, most of us want our liturgies (the rituals we do in church) to be based on sound ideas about God. That is, we give priority to theology over ritual.

The idea of "ritual," then, is a problem for many of us. If Christian rituals are nothing more than expressions of theological ideas, then why not share the ideas without the ritual? Why can't we rely on spontaneous expressions of our beliefs rather than repeating rituals that few of us fully understand?

But let's be honest. Is total spontaneity in worship really possible? We could rarely make up our hymns on the spot, and even if we did, no one could sing them with us. We might give up all printed prayers and only offer prayer extemporaneously. What, however, makes any of our utterances *sound* like prayers if we do not use familiar patterns (…in the name of Jesus; O God…; Lord, we just want to…)? The obvious conclusion is that we will always have ritual in our worship, because without it we would not have the structures necessary to call what we do Christian worship. Actually, even those who eschew all fixed liturgies, such as the Quakers, have a highly disciplined and structured type of worship, which is actually another form of ritual. The option is not between having rituals or having no rituals; the option is between acknowledging our rituals or denying their claim on us.

Rituals evolve as we make changes to them over time. Nevertheless, such changes only become ritual when they are repeated over time. Furthermore, they are repeated over time when they can somehow work within the ritual patterns that already have been established. We may alter our rituals, but we will never be able to simply make them up out of thin air. It is the essence of ritual that it is something we *receive*, rather than something we *create*.[14] We continue to practice our rituals as long as they generate some sort of meaning for us; when they cease to generate meaning we slowly abandon them or give them new meanings.

WORSHIP AS WORD

Once we acknowledge that all worship will necessarily involve ritual, the question that confronts us is: how do we know that our rituals are good for us? How can we evaluate them? How do we know that the meanings they generate within us are fit for Christian worship? The Protestant reformers of the sixteenth century claimed that our understanding of the Word of God as found in the scriptures, establishes proper liturgy, and they initiated attempts at reforming worship based on sound, biblical theology. Therefore, the answer that Protestants typically will give to these questions is: "Worship (and its rituals) is faithful to its task when it expresses the Word of God in Jesus Christ." In other words, worship is an act of the Word of God, and we evaluate our worship rituals according to our understanding of the Word of God: theology establishes the practice of worship.

The church in the Middle Ages used a different principle to describe the relationship between worship rituals and theology: "The rule of prayer establishes the rule of belief."[15] That is to say, worship is the primary source of our theology since worship is the place where God addresses us through proclamation and sacrament, and where we respond to God through prayer and praise. We know our theology is sound when we as a community find it congruent with and productive for our experience of prayer: worship practice establishes theology.

These two ways of understanding the relationship of theology and worship (theology establishes worship, or worship establishes theology) may seem to oppose each other. The Methodist theologian, Geoffrey Wainwright, has pointed out, however, that both of these principles operate in the history of the church. Liturgy gives rise to theology, which then is used to critique and reform liturgy, which generates renewed theology, causing us to reconsider our liturgy, and so on.[16]

Let us propose another metaphor for understanding the relationship between the rituals of worship and theology: liturgical rituals are like icebergs. Much of an iceberg is below the surface of the ocean, out of sight; only part of it is visible. We know the depth is there even though we see only a small tip. Similarly, much of the meaning of liturgical ritual is hidden deep within our tradition, within our collective memories, within the mystery of God in Jesus Christ. Part of it is knowable and understandable—the part above the surface. We must have some knowledge and understanding of the part we can "see" or else we have no reason to believe that there is anything in the depths below. We can never comprehend all the meaning given within our liturgy, no matter how detailed our theological analysis may be. Nevertheless, the part that we can comprehend should be as clear and shimmering as the top of a massive iceberg. Mystery without meaning is merely confusion. Worship, therefore, is not only ritual, it is also enacted "word"; we must be able to comprehend it as an expression of the Word of God.

WORSHIP AS WORLDVIEW

Christian worship, then, is a ritual that "enacts" the Word of God. There is one more dimension to the action of worship: it embodies a worldview. Worship through ritual, prayer, praise, and proclamation, gives us a way of seeing the world as a whole. It incorporates us into a master story, the Good News of Jesus Christ. This story begins with creation of the world and its estrangement from God through sin, and it continues through God's calling of Israel to be a light to the nations. The story finds its center in the life, death and resurrection of Jesus Christ. It continues up to the present through Christ's Lordship within the Church, and looks with hope toward the consummation of Christ's reign in the renewal of the earth and a healing of the world's estrangement from God.

Christian worship is an enacted, embodied worldview, because in our worship through ritual and word we rehearse again and again this amazing, historical story of God's relationship to the world, which clashes with alternative constructions of reality that do not know this historical God. In other words, our worship lets us see our world as it really is, despite all appearances to the contrary. We will say more about how worship gives shape to this particular Christian worldview. But here it will suffice to say that the worldview of our worship must function on all the levels of our master story - catholic, denominational, local, and personal - if we are to be thoroughly shaped by it. For this is how the cosmic story of God becomes incarnate in those of us who are the Body of Christ in this place, here and now.

WORSHIP: EMPOWERED BY THE HOLY SPIRIT

We have said that Christian worship is ritual that expresses the Word of God in Jesus Christ and grounds us in the story of God's history with the world. There is more to our definition. In worship, God empowers us by the Holy Spirit to live this story in the world as witnesses to God's love. Jesus says to his disciples in the Book of Acts: "You will receive power when the Holy Spirit has come upon you, and you shall be my witnesses in Jerusalem, in all Judea and Samaria, and to the ends of the earth" (Acts 1:8). By the power of the Holy Spirit at Pentecost, ordinary men and women were changed into apostles and missionaries, spreading the Gospel throughout the Roman Empire and beyond. They became the corporate body of Christ, continuing his work in the world of proclaiming good news to the poor and release of prisoners, healing of the blind, and freeing of the oppressed.

The powerful presence of the Holy Spirit, which we encounter in our worship, changes things. Water becomes the washing away of our old life and the birth of new life. Bread and wine become the body and blood of Jesus Christ to nourish us for that new life. Ordinary women and men today are still transformed into Christ's body to continue his work in the world. When Christians gather for worship, we become lightening rods for God to strike the earth with the energy of new creation. God, of course, could do this apart from our gathering for worship. In our common worship, however, God through Christ has specifically promised to meet us in our offering of prayer and celebration of sacrament. These ritual actions, therefore, are what John Wesley called instituted means of grace. Through them the Holy Spirit converts us, sanctifies us and perfects us in love—love for God and for the world. When our worship is empowered by the Holy Spirit, we learn how to be the Body of Christ in service to all of God's wounded creation—not only to human beings, but also to the whole planet. We become God's agents for the renewal of the earth, the New Creation.

WORSHIP: PAST, PRESENT, AND FUTURE

We began this chapter with the observation that dissatisfaction with worship arises from our longing for deeper faithfulness. We suggested further that attempts to reform worship that rely exclusively on either "traditional" or "contemporary" models are not adequate solutions to our longing for more faithful worship. This actually is a false dichotomy since authentic Christian worship is by necessity *both* contemporary and traditional. It is traditional because it must continue the story of Jesus Christ in the world in history, and it is contemporary because it must be engaged with the present, with actual people who live in particular cultures. Authentic worship, however, not only continues the tradition and engages the present; it also anticipates the future of God's coming New

Creation. It is this cosmic renewal of heaven and earth that God begins to work in us whenever we gather to worship and continue the story of Jesus Christ in the power of the Spirit. That is the truth of our worship.

ENDNOTES

[1] "For the Spirit of Truth," from Kenya, *UMH*, 597.

[2] Timothy Wright, *A Community of Joy: How to Create Contemporary Worship* (Nashville: Abingdon, 1994) 30-34.

[3] Wright, 19-23.

[4] Wright, 55.

[5] John Polkinghorne, *Science and Christian Belief: Theological Reflections of a Bottom-Up Thinker* (London: Society for Promoting Christian Knowledge, 1994) 30ff.

[6] See George Lindbeck, *The Nature of Doctrine* (Philadelphia: Westminster Press, 1984) 30-45.

[7] This observation is central to much of the writing of United Methodist Theologian Stanley Hauerwas. See, for example, chapter one of his book written with fellow United Methodist William Willimon, *Resident Aliens* (Nashville: Abingdon, 1989). See also William C. Placher, *Unapologetic Theology* (Louisville: Westminster/John Knox Press, 1989) 24-38.

[8] Jane Wagner, *The Search for Signs of Intelligent Life in the Universe* (New York: Harper and Row, 1986) 88.

[9] See Neil Postman, *Amusing Ourselves to Death: Public Discourse in the Age of Show Business* (New York: Penguin Books, 1985).

[10] Marianne Sawicki makes this point in her essay, "How can Christian Worship be contemporary?" in *What is "contemporary" worship?*, Gordon Lathrop, ed. (Minneapolis: Augsburg Fortress, 1995) 22-31.

[11] To this day, all United Methodist clergy must promise to strive for Christian Perfection as part of their ordination examination.

[12] Pierre Bourdieu, *The Logic of Practice*, Richard Nice, trans. (Stanford: Stanford University Press, 1990), 17-19; 66-73.

[13] See Frank Senn, *Christian Liturgy: Catholic and Evangelical* (Minneapolis: Fortress Press, 1997) 3-4.

[14] Roy Rappaport, *Ritual and Religion in the Making of Humanity* (Cambridge: Cambridge University Press, 1999) 132.

[15] *Lex orandi, lex credendi*, an expression attributed to Prosper of Aquitaine in the sixth century.

[16] Geoffrey Wainwright, *Doxology: The Practice of God in Worship, Doctrine, and Life* (New York: Oxford University Press, 1980) 218-9.

Chapter Two

In Spirit and Truth

We believe, O Lord, that you have not abandoned us
to the dim light of our own reason to conduct us to happiness,
but that you have revealed in Holy Scriptures
whatever is necessary for us to believe and practice.[1]

Richard Allen,
First African American Episcopal bishop

In the previous chapter, we claim that faithful worship is the way God forms us in the practice of living according to the Truth. We also indicate that "Truth" means seeing the world as it "really is" and not as a "virtual" reality. Now we will examine five biblical passages that indicate how faithful worship involves seeing the world as it really is — that is, to see the world as revealed by the life, death and resurrection of Jesus Christ. We believe these passages represent a foundation of truth crucial for authentic renewal of faithful worship in the twenty-first century.

SCRIPTURAL UNDERSTANDING OF TRUTH-FULL WORSHIP
JOHN 4:1-30: WORSHIP AS SPIRITUAL TRUTH

The theme of "seeing clearly" dominates the Gospel of John from its opening verses. Jesus Christ, the Word made flesh, as John tells us, is the "true light," which enlightens the world (John 1:9). We may think that light by definition would be the most obvious phenomenon possible. Yet, paradoxically, John indicates that the world does not see this light. When Jesus works his miraculous signs or encounters persons in his ministry, almost always people misunderstand what is actually taking place or being said. Jesus changes water into wine, and the chief steward thinks there has been a mistake in catering the wedding, since the best was saved for last. Jesus heals a man born blind, and the blindness of the Pharisees hinders their ability to see this as a sign from God. Jesus tells Nicodemus that he must be born from above, and Nicodemus makes the ridiculous mistake of thinking Jesus has suggested he climb back into his mother's womb. Jesus tells Pilate that he has come to testify to the truth, and Pilate asks, "What's that?" According to the Gospel of John, the light or the truth, which should be obvious, is not obvious because people are caught up in a blinding darkness. This blindness has nothing to do with the physical ability to see.

The story of the Samaritan Woman at the Well in John 4 is a typical illustration of the spiritual blindness that Jesus exposes. In the story, Jesus is left alone at a well while his disciples go into a town to get food. A lone woman comes to the well in the middle of the day to draw water. There are at least three points of dramatic tension in this encounter. First, the woman is a Samaritan, and Jews did not, as a rule, associate with Samaritans. Second, the Samaritan is a woman, and Jewish men did not, as a rule, associate with women to whom they were not related. Third, this particular Samaritan woman was an acknowledged sinner, and rabbis did not, as a rule, associate with acknowledged sinners. No doubt, the reason that the woman comes alone to the well in the heat of the noonday sun is that even the other women of her own village do not want to associate with her. Therefore, the woman is understandably surprised when Jesus asks her for a drink.

Then Jesus surprises her even further by offering her "living water." This living water is the revelation that Jesus himself gives.[2] The woman at first completely misunderstands and thinks that Jesus is, perhaps, pulling her leg — "What living water? You don't even have a bucket." And later, "Living water? Great, give me some so I won't have to keep coming back out here to this well."

Eventually the conversation begins to turn more serious when Jesus asks about the woman's husband. The woman tells Jesus she is not married, but Jesus has already discerned that her relationship to men has been personally disastrous. "You have had five husbands," he says, "but you are not married to the man with whom you now live." The woman abruptly changes the subject (who wouldn't!) to the theological dispute between Jews and Samaritans concerning the proper worship: "Where is the better place to worship God? In Samaria or in Jerusalem?" Jesus responds: "The hour is coming when you will worship the Father neither on this mountain nor in Jerusalem...But the hour is coming, and is now here, when the true worshipers will worship the Father in spirit and truth...." The woman responds, "The Messiah who is coming will tell us all these things," meaning that the Messiah will tell what the truth is. Jesus responds, "I am he" (John 4:21, 23, 25-26).

What does Jesus mean by the phrase, "worship the Father in spirit and truth"? In a later passage, John 16:4-15, Jesus refers to "the Spirit of Truth," which is the Holy Spirit that he will send upon the disciples as an Advocate or Helper after the resurrection and ascension. Jesus tells the disciples that this Advocate will "prove the world wrong about sin and righteousness and judgment: about sin, because they do not believe in me; about righteousness, because I am going to the Father and you will see me no longer; about judgment, because the ruler of this world has been condemned" (John 16:8b-11). Clearly, therefore, to worship in spirit and truth does not mean to worship in some sort of internal or private "spiritual" manner as opposed to the public worship of the Jews or Samaritans. Spiritual worship is not opposed to life in the created world *per se,* but to the systems of the *fallen* world—the world that has an impaired ability to see sin, righteousness and judgment. Jesus indicates that the world is wrong about sin and righteousness when it judges him to be a sinner because he breaks the Sabbath, or associates with disreputable people, or arouses the suspicions of the government. The one who heals on the Sabbath, who does not separate himself from Samaritans or women, and who refuses to be afraid of the authority of Rome is not a sinner, but on the contrary, is the one who lives in complete fellowship with God.

To see the world truly, therefore, is to understand that the one who has been crucified and raised is the one who is the "way, the truth, and the life." In the story of the Samaritan woman, it means, at the very least, that the way we tend to divide the world up into "our kind and their kind," the "pure and the impure," the "acceptable and the outcast," is the way of a world caught up in darkness, unable to see the light. True worshipers, Jesus claims, will worship in a way that overcomes these divisions.

ROMANS 12: WORSHIP AS EMBODIED COMMUNITY

In Romans 12, Paul gives us a concrete picture of what it means to worship in spirit and truth; it involves our *bodies.* "I appeal to you therefore, brothers and sisters, by the mercies of God, to present your bodies as a living sacrifice, holy and acceptable to God, which is your spiritual (or reasonable) worship" (Romans 12:1). When Paul tells the Romans to present their "bodies as a living sacrifice," he is contrasting the worship of the Christian with the animal sacrifices in the Temple at Jerusalem. We might see an allusion here to the words of Micah 6:6-8: "With what shall I come before the Lord, and bow myself before God on high? Shall I come before him with burnt offerings? ...He has told you, O mortal, what is good; and what does the Lord require of you but to do justice, and to love kindness, and to walk humbly with your God." Or, perhaps Paul is alluding to Psalm 51:17 "The sacrifice acceptable to God is a broken spirit." The point here is that Paul is defining Christian worship within the sacrificial tradition of the Old Testament, but especially the part of the tradition that stresses the ethical life of the worshiper.

The "living sacrifice" of the Christian's body is "spiritual worship" or "reasonable" worship. The phrase is a little difficult to translate, though "reasonable" may be the better translation. The word in Greek is *logike'* and it is related to the Greek word *logos* or "word." This is the term which the Gospel of John uses when it begins, "In the beginning was the Word (*logos*)..." As a Greek philosophical term, *logos* is the invisible structure or order in the universe, the "logic" which holds things in place. Therefore, this "reasonable" worship of the body is not "spiritual" in some otherworldly sense. Rather, it is worship that is grounded in the invisible, but very real structures of the universe—the world as it really is, not simply as it appears to be.

Paul elaborates this concept of "reasonable worship" in the following verse, Romans 12:2: "Do not be conformed to this world, but be transformed by the renewing of your minds, so that you may discern what is the will of God—what is good and acceptable and perfect." Reasonable worship with our bodies involves a transformed mind—that is, a transformed way of seeing the world. For Paul, conformity to the world is "living in the darkness" which Jesus talks about in the Gospel of John. Reasonable worship means seeing the world in the light of Jesus Christ, for only then can we know what is "good, acceptable and perfect," God's view of the world as it really is.

In the rest of Romans 12 and in the following chapter, Paul gives concrete directions how to embody this reasonable worship: "Let love be genuine, be patient in suffering, contribute to the saints, bless those who persecute you, do not repay anyone evil for evil, live peaceably with all, do not overcome evil with evil, but overcome evil with good," and so on.[3] Furthermore, this embodied worship involves more than our individual bodies: "so we, who are many, are one body in Christ, and individually we are members one of another" (Romans 12:5).

Paul even meddles in things that we might think of as very "worldly" matters: "Pay to all what is due them—taxes to whom taxes are due, respect to whom respect is due, honor to whom honor is due" (Romans 13:7). But, even here there is a logic that runs counter to the world's view of these matters: "Owe no one anything, except to love one another; for the one who loves another has fulfilled the law" (Romans 13:8). Paying taxes as an expression of Christian love? Surely that requires a radically different view of the world. Yet for Paul, just such a renewed mind is what is required for us to present our bodies as a reasonable sacrifice of Spirit-filled worship. *Our sacrifice requires that our life and work in the world conform to our worship, not that our worship conform to the world.*

1 CORINTHIANS 11: WORSHIP AS EATING TOGETHER

Paul addresses the gathered worship life of the community more directly in 1 Corinthians 11: 17-34. In this passage, Paul specifically criticizes the Corinthians' practice of the Lord's Supper. This is one of four texts in the New Testament which refer to Jesus' own words of institution as the foundation for the Christian Lord's Supper.[4] Paul adds his own comment: "For as often as you eat this bread and drink the cup, you proclaim the Lord's death until he comes" (1 Corinthians 11:26). Yet only a few verses earlier, Paul has told the Corinthians that they are not really eating the Lord's Supper because their meal practice is horribly divisive: "For when the time comes to eat, each of you goes ahead with your own supper, and one goes hungry and another becomes drunk" (1 Corinthians 11:21). Obviously, at this time, Christians celebrated the Lord's Supper in the context of a full fellowship meal, rather than the symbolic meal that Christians practice today. In the social organization of the early house churches, these communal meals were important for the formation of the church as a family. However, at Corinth, the more affluent members of the church, who would be able to bring most of the food, would go ahead and begin eating. Those who were servants or slaves, or who "punched a clock," got to the gatherings later, and often there was nothing left for them to eat. The scandal here, Paul indicates, is that such behavior stratifies the community into rich and poor, free and slave. When the Corinthians allow this *practice of dividing the community* they are not discerning the *body of Jesus* (1 Corinthians 11:29). For eating and drinking together as one family, rich and poor, slave and free, *is the essential sacramental sign* of Jesus' new covenant. Thus, in 1 Cor. 10: 17, Paul says, "Because there is one bread, we who are many are one body, for we all partake of the one bread." To the degree that the church does not do this, it is not demonstrating the body of Jesus in the world in its sacramental fellowship of the Lord's Supper.

According to Paul, the actual social practice of this very real community of believers has tremendous spiritual significance. As in Romans 12, the offering of our bodies is our reasonable, logical, spiritual worship. Our physical bodies are the concrete location points of the corporate Body of Christ, for what we Christians do as individual bodies we also and always do as members of the Body.[5]

The importance of the Body of Christ as the primary identity for Christians means that Christian prayer and worship are always corporate worship. Jesus instructed them to pray "*Our* Father in heaven," rather than "*My* Father" (Matthew 6:9). This does not mean that Christians should forsake devotional prayer, but only that the primary center of prayer is the Christian community. We are individual members of the Body of Christ; we always pray as a group, even when we are alone.

1 Corinthians 14: Worship as Orderly Community

The same church that had members who did not want to wait for others in order to begin their fellowship meals, also had members who did not care whether their personal worship habits were edifying for the community. This passage is difficult for some Christians today (while others are very attracted to it) because it deals with a controversial Christian practice, that of speaking in tongues. We should notice that Paul himself claims to speak in tongues, even more than the Corinthians, so we cannot suggest that he disapproved of the practice. However, he does indicate that it must come under the discipline of the community. If a Christian speaks out loud in an unknown tongue, someone must interpret what he or she is saying. Otherwise, this person should be silent. Paul does not have much patience for those who claim not to be able to contain their ecstatic outbursts: "The spirits of the prophets are subject to the prophets" (1 Corinthians 14: 32). In other words, we have control over our prayers. We can control ourselves in worship.

The Corinthians appear to have wanted to interpret all of the chaotic, individualist, ecstatic praying and shouting in their worship gatherings as amazing signs of the presence of the Holy Spirit among them. It is not unlike the dilemma we face today, with so many speaking loudly and insistently about their way as the valid movement of the Holy Spirit, wanting their *own* tongues to be heard! Nowhere is this more evident in mainstream Protestant churches than in worship renewal. Some voices say their music is the only way, others speak of style and atmosphere, and others defend or denounce various liturgical practices. Many of these positions are similar to the individualistic and divisive practices of the Corinthian church.

Rather than encouraging enthusiastic, individualistic chaos, Paul writes, "God is a God not of disorder but of peace" (1 Corinthians 14:33). What he does, specifically, is give the Corinthians an "Order of Worship:" "What would be done then, my friends? When you come together, each one has a hymn, a lesson, a revelation, a tongue, or an interpretation. Let all things be done for building up" (1 Corinthians 14:26). Paul does not want to quash enthusiasm, *per se*; he merely wants to discipline the personal worship habits of the individuals in the Corinthian church for the sake of the community: "So, my friends, be eager to prophesy, and do not forbid speaking in tongues; but all things should be done decently and in order" (1 Corinthians 14:39-40).

We must comment on two verses in 1 Corinthians 14, which over the centuries have been given a problematic interpretation. "As in all the church of the saints, women should be silent in the churches. For they are not permitted to speak, but should be subordinate, as the law also says. If there is any thing they desire to know, let them ask their husbands at home. For it is shameful for a woman to speak in church. Or did the word of God originate with you? Or are you the only ones it has reached?" (1 Corinthians 14: 33a-36). What does Paul mean here? Is Paul merely being a "controlling" male chauvinist? Probably not in the way he has been charged with it, since, in 1 Corinthians 11: 5, Paul acknowledges that there are women prophets in the Corinthian community. How can women prophesy and at the same time "remain silent"? Obviously, Paul is not giving some categorical rule that women should never speak in worship. We suggest, rather, that what Paul is doing is *affirming* the public role of women in the church by saying that the *rules of community order* apply to them as well as to men. Since there are women in the church who prophesy, and we may assume also speak in tongues, Paul is insisting that they must keep quiet *like everyone else* in the community unless it is their turn to speak.

Perhaps an example is in order. Imagine a parent who whispers to an unruly child in worship (not difficult to picture), "You need to be quiet in this service so you won't distract people in worship." "Fine," says the child. A few minutes later, the whole congregation rises to sing a hymn, and the child remains quietly seated with arms folded. The parent again whispers, "Aren't you going to sing?" The child responds: "You TOLD me to be quiet!"

In a very similar way, when Paul instructs the Corinthian women to be silent in worship, he does not mean, "Silent always, unlike all the men who are allowed to speak out." Rather, he means, "Silent, when appropriate, waiting their turn to speak, just like the men." That is, Paul's concern here is to curb the individualistic, idiosyncratic, chaotic worship of the Corinthians in favor of a worship which demonstrates order, peace, and understanding: embodied worship appropriate to the corporate Body of Christ. All of these issues reiterate Paul's primary definition: "Present your bodies as a living sacrifice, holy and acceptable to God, which is your reasonable worship."

Worship for the New Testament church therefore is always about the big picture: seeing the world "in spirit and truth" as

Jesus says in the Gospel of John, or about "discerning the good, acceptable and perfect will of God," as Paul says in Romans. It is about spirit and it is about body (both individual and corporate), thoroughly connected as the two aspects of the Christian's life. As we say in the previous chapter, worship is a ritual (involves the body) and a word (involves spiritual understanding and meaning).

The Book of Revelation:
Worship in a New Heaven and New Earth

Finally, worship involves a radically new worldview. We have already indicated how the Gospel of John and Paul present this radically different, and not easily discernable, worldview. No place in the New Testament indicates the importance of worship in this radically different worldview more than the Revelation to John.

John of Patmos declares that he was "in the spirit on the Lord's Day" (Revelation 1:10) when he received the Revelation. The "Lord's Day" was an early Christian word for Sunday. The Lord's Day was the weekly commemoration of the resurrection of Jesus, and almost certainly was a day when Christians shared in the Lord's Supper.[6]   John explicitly mentions that the revelation came to him on "the Lord's Day." This connects his vision of heaven with the weekly Sunday worship of the Christian churches of Patmos and Asia Minor.

The Greek word *apocalypse* and the English word "revelation" indicate that something is going to be "revealed" or "uncovered." We might find this somewhat ironic since so much of the Revelation to John strikes us as very difficult or even impossible to understand. No doubt, when John first wrote down his vision, he used code words, images, and allusions that he knew his fellow Christians in Asia Minor would understand, but which are very obscure or ambiguous to us many centuries later. This ambiguity has allowed the Revelation to be interpreted in all sorts of fantastical ways in order to make it relevant to our own age. John has been credited with foreseeing the invention of modern fighter planes, nuclear bombs, and computer technology. Candidates for the "Antichrist" have included popes, European dictators, U.S. presidents, and even a certain computer software manufacturer.

The problem with such specific one-to-one interpretations is they imply that God gave a revelation to John that was totally obscure to him and his fellow Christians, but which is now becoming obvious to us. Furthermore, such an approach disregards the worship setting for the vision. We would rather suggest that the Revelation to John is about how worship enables us to see more clearly what God has been up to in the world *in every age* between the first coming of Jesus and the second coming of Jesus.

The Revelation gives us insight into how the world of the spirit (the divine realm) corresponds to the world of the here-and-now. Thus, when Christ instructs John to send letters to the seven churches in Asia Minor, the letters are addressed to the "angels" of the churches. These seven "angels" are represented by seven "stars," indicating their heavenly location (Revelation 1:20). The seven churches on earth correspond to seven specific angels in heaven.

After two chapters in which John is given the letters, he is shown a door that opens into heaven. What does John see? A magnificent vision of worship! God is seated on a throne, shining like a rainbow of jewels. Surrounding God are twenty-four thrones with twenty-four "elders" seated on them. One conventional interpretation is that these elders represent the twelve patriarchs of the tribes of Israel together with the twelve Apostles of Jesus Christ—the people of the Old and New covenants added together. Be that as it may, they certainly represent the saints of God since they are dressed in white robes and are wearing crowns. In addition to these elders, John sees four angelic beings similar to the angelic figures that the prophet Ezekiel beholds in his first vision (Ezekiel 1:17-25), and similar to the Seraphim which Isaiah sees in his vision of the heavenly throne room (Isaiah 6:2-3).

These different forms of angelic beings depict a comprehensive heavenly representation of all living land creatures: lions = wild animals; oxen = domestic animals; human face =

human beings; eagle = flying animals. These angelic beings, representing all creation, fly around the throne of God singing "Holy, holy, holy, the Lord God the Almighty, who was and is and is to come" (Revelation 4:8). The twenty-four elders "cast their crowns before the throne, singing, 'You are worthy, our Lord and God to receive glory and honor and power, for you created all things, and by your will they existed and were created'" (Revelation 4:10b-11).

One of the great hymns of our church puts this scene from Revelation to music:

> Holy, holy, holy, Lord God Almighty,
> Early in the morning our song shall rise to thee…
> Holy, holy, holy, all the saints adore thee,
> Casting down their golden crowns around the glassy sea,
> Cheribim and Seraphim, falling down before Thee,
> Which wert and art and evermore shall be.[7]

Whenever Christians sing this popular text hymn we acknowledge the connection of our worship here on earth with the heavenly worship described by John. We may not actually "see" the "living creatures" and "twenty-four elders" but we know that they are there always representing us in the presence of God, forever worshiping the one "who is seated on the throne."

God in heaven holds a scroll, which seems to represent God's plan for the world, but no one is found worthy to open the scroll—no one except the "Lion of the tribe of Judah," who "has conquered" (Revelation 5:5). However, when John looks to see this "conquering Lion," instead of a lion he sees "a Lamb standing as if it had been slain" (Revelation 5:6). This is one of many paradoxes in the Revelation to John. The one who is worthy "to receive power and wealth and wisdom and might and honor and glory and blessing" is the "Lamb that was slaughtered" (Revelation 5:12). The rest of the revelation gives us a heavenly picture of how the people of God will conquer Satan (represented by a dragon) "by the blood of the Lamb and by the word of their testimony" (Revelation 12:11).

This victory will not be easy for them, and John indicates that the struggle will be a conflict in worship: either God and the Lamb, or Satan and the beast. Revelation 12 describes a war in heaven in which Satan and his angels are defeated by the angels of God. Satan is cast down to earth to make war on the saints. Once on earth, Satan raises up a beast out the sea (note that the angels who surround God's throne look like land creatures, while Satan and his angel get the stormy oceans) who will blasphemously require the sort of worshipful alliegiance due to God alone. Those who refuse to worship "the beast" are threatened with death.

What is the problem with the beast? The beast represents what New Testament scholar Walter Wink has called "the Domination System," the way of a fallen world in which violence is used to maintain the divisions of class and privilege.[8] The kings of the nations and merchants who benefit from exploitation of the poor are the ones who weep when the beast is finally destroyed. However, the very violence and exploitation that the "beast" uses to maintain its power and demand its worship contain the seeds of the "beast's" own destruction.

The idea of Roman economic exploitation is not something that only became a problem in the first century when John wrote down the Revelation. Indeed, in addition to calling the Domination System a "beast," he refers to that system as "Babylon." For John, Babylon was a code word for Rome, which was the superpower in his day, just as Babylon was the super power in the sixth century B.C. Thus Babylon, like the "beast," is really a code word for all systems of domination in our fallen world. All governments who rule by the sword and all economic systems that rule through exploitation are "Babylon."

According to the Revelation, so comprehensive and powerful is this Domination System that the temptation to worship the beast is nearly irresistable: "who is like the beast, and who can fight against it?" (Revelevation 13:4). Yet, John calls for "endurance and faith of the saints." And he tells Christians to separate themselves from the abusive systems around them: "Come out of her, my people, so that you do not take part in her sins, and so that you do not share in her plagues..." (Revelation 18:4).

The conflict which the Revelation puts before us is, therefore, a conflict in worship: worship the dominating beast or worship the slain Lamb by becoming a witness to the power of the Cross. Nevertheless, it would be a mistake to think that John believes God wants a total withdrawal from the world around us. The world is fallen, but God has great plans for restoration and redemption. In Revelation 21 we have a picture of what God intends to be the culmination of history: a new heaven and earth, in which there is no more violence, death or sorrow. In this new heaven and earth, described as a "New Jerusalem," God dwells so completely and manifestly that there is no need for a temple in which to worship—the entire city has become a temple to God. There will be no need of sun or moon, for the Glory of God will be the light (Revelation 21.22-23). What God intends is a world that functions as it was created to function: "the nations will walk by its light, and the kings of the earth will bring their glory into it. Its gates will never be shut by day, and there will be no night there. People will bring into it the glory and honor of the nations" (Revelation 21:24-26). Contrary to what the world thinks, John tells us, the power of the sword is not the glory of the nations, nor is death the ultimate mark of honor. Rather, the glory and honor of the nations is a future of peace and abundance, with no more domination by death, poverty or privilege.

All this (and much more than this brief overview of the Revelation could develop) John saw while at worship one Sunday morning on the Island of Patmos. He caught a vision of the world as "it really is" in the light of what God intends the world to be. For John, worship was a powerfully enacted "worldview," which provides us with a model of what it means to worship "in spirit and truth."

To summarize, the New Testament offers us an understanding of worship renewal that is embodied in real people and communities, not in some unobtainable image of spiritual perfection. Furthermore, the Christian community at the core of worship is not merely a group of individuals, each doing his or her own thing, but rather, a harmoniously diverse body of women and men, Samaritan and Jew, the strong and the weak, young and old, each contributing distinctive gifts to the worship of God. Such worship exposes as false any ritual that is not rooted in ethical living. Finally, the New Testament demonstrates how worship connects us to the real world that is the world as God intends rather than the fallen world and its structures of violence and division. Thus the scriptural testimony sets the stage for renewal of our worship practice "in spirit and in truth."

The church that understands and practices worship in the model of the New Testament will see that it is connected with the whole of salvation history, that there is a cloud of witnesses who have gone before, and that God's spirit will empower us for struggles to come. Or, to put it another way, such a practice of worship will result in strong faith communities that can discern between the reality and the "virtual reality" of the culture around them.

WORSHIP IN SPIRIT AND IN TRUTH

What the Bible does not tell us is how a typical worship service would look in one of Paul's churches, or how the Christians in Jerusalem structured their prayers, or what the church of Patmos was doing when John received his revelation. We can speculate that the early Christians in Jerusalem conducted their services along the same lines as the Jews of the day, since they were still Jews themselves, but we do not know what Jews *did* in their synagogues in the first century. No complete order of service has survived from the time of Jesus, either Jewish or Christian.

What we can piece together is that Christians prayed, read scripture (for the New Testament church this meant the Old Testament, of course), recalled the words and deeds of Jesus (Paul quotes Jesus in a sermon in Acts 20:35), preached, and ate the Lord's Supper together every week. Sound familiar? The simple fact that Christian worship still contains all of these elements in the twenty-first century is testimony to the power of the tradition.

ENDNOTES

[1] *The United Methodist Book of Worship* (Nashville: The United Methodist Publishing House, 1992) 461.

[2] God's wisdom, for example, is compared to a flowing fountain in Proverbs 13: 14, and in Proverbs 18:4. See, Raymond E. Brown, *The Gospel According to John*, The Anchor Bible, Vol. 29A, (New York: Doubleday & Co., 1966) 178.

[3] Excerpts from Romans 12:9-21.

[4] The other three texts are Matthew 26:26-29, Mark 14:22-25, and Luke 22:15-20.

[5] Paul provides his most thorough description of the church as the Body of Christ in 1 Corinthians 12.

[6] See Acts 20:7.

[7] Reginald Heber, "Holy, Holy, Holy, Lord God Almighty," *UMH* 64.

[8] Walter Wink, *Engaging the Powers* (Minneapolis: Fortress Press, 1992) 87-104.

Chapter Three

With the Entire Company of Heaven

O blest communion, fellowship divine!
We feebly struggle, they in glory shine;
yet all are one in thee, for all are thine.
Alleluia, Alleluia![1]

At the conclusion of chapter two, we described how John received the Revelation at Sunday worship and suggested that such revelation is an essential function of our worship that enables us to see the world as it is from God's point of view. There is a passage in the United Methodist Ritual for the Lord's Supper that alludes to the Revelation to John and illustrates another important aspect of Christian worship. Worship connects us with all creatures, in all times and places, who worship God.

And so, with your people on earth
and all the company of heaven,
we praise your name and join in their unending hymn, singing,
"Holy, holy, holy, Lord, God of power and might,
heaven and earth are full of your glory..."[2]

This passage is absolutely stunning in its affirmation of the universal significance of our worship. The "entire company of heaven" refers to the elders and the living creatures, and the other angels and saints who worship God day and night, those whom John saw in his vision of the heavenly throne-room. "All your people on earth," refers to all Christians everywhere who are also offering their worship of God. The hymn which the congregation sings makes the point of connecting our worship on earth with the worship of angels in heaven, for we sing the same song, "Holy, holy, holy, Lord God Almighty..." (cf. Revelation 4:8). Thus, in this short passage from our Ritual we have an amazing affirmation of the universal and eternal significance of our worship whenever any United Methodist congregation offers this prayer in the celebration of the Lord's Supper. Worship is not something that we simply make happen in our local setting; rather, it is already going on all around us, in heaven among the angels and saints, on earth wherever Christians worship, past, present and future. When we worship, we add our voice to that universal, eternal song of praise. As the Ritual says, "we join their *unending* hymn."

We should note here that this passage from the Great Thanksgiving of the Ritual for Holy Communion in *The United Methodist Hymnal* is certainly not unique to United Methodists. Christians have used words very similar to this in celebrations of the Lord's Supper since *at least* the fourth century A.D. We suspect that this short passage in our Ritual has been read countless times with very few of us realizing what an amazing thing we are claiming. Not only is it impossible for Christians to worship as individuals (remember, Jesus taught us to say "*Our* Father in heaven..."), it is impossible for us to worship as separate congregations. Christian worship is not merely "communal;" it is also always "catholic" or "universal."

To say that Christian worship is universal does not mean that it has been the same at all times and places, nor does it mean that there ought to be absolute conformity in worship throughout the world. Indeed, as we examine the history of Christian worship, we see that worship changes over the years, and from location to location because worship is a living practice, and all living things change. Furthermore, there is a rich diversity among various human cultures in which Christians find themselves. Art, music, language, architecture, communication, transportation and other aspects of culture inevitably engage the Christian church at worship since these are aspects of culture which Christians share with those outside of the church. Nevertheless, underneath the many diverse cultural or denominational expressions of Christian worship we should always be able to discern an essential connection to the universal worship of God by the saints in heaven and around the whole earth. Such worship expresses our fundamental Christian identity, because worshiping God is what the saints do. *This universal praise is our fundamental reality.*

There will always be a dynamic tension between the fundamental reality of our worship and the typical expressions of our worship in any congregation. This is why, as we said earlier, the church will always be engaged in the process of worship renewal. In this chapter we will examine a few important voices from the history of the church to see how Christians after the New Testament period have understood the fundamental reality of the worship of the saints as the source for Christian worship and life in the world.

Worship in the Early Church

During the first centuries of its existence, the church remained under threat of persecution, which forced it to be a relatively low-key movement. Consequently, the church grew as small cell groups or house churches which were organized into a sort of federation among the various cities and regions of the Roman Empire and beyond. This worship was not generally public, in the sense that we think of public worship today with the church at the corner of Main and Vine. Certainly there is no evidence that the early church used its worship as a means for evangelization. Rather, worship was an "underground" activity, and outsiders were admitted into the church only when a church member could vouch for them.

What did the Christians do when they gathered for worship? The earliest detailed description of Christian worship comes from Justin Martyr, a Christian at Rome who writes a treatise to explain Christianity to the pagan world.[3] In his *First Apology* which dates from around the year 150 A.D., Justin gives two brief overviews of the content of Christian worship. In the first account, Justin describes the celebration of the Lord's Supper, which follows a baptism service:

> Having ended the prayers [the intercessions], we greet one another with a kiss. There is then brought to the president of the brothers and sisters bread and a cup of wine mixed with water; and he taking them, gives praise and glory to the Father of the universe, through the name of the Son and of the Holy Spirit, and offers thanks at considerable length for our being counted worthy to receive these things from him. [4]

In the second account, Justin gives a somewhat more complete order of Sunday worship that does not include baptism:

> And on the day called Sunday, all who live in cities or in the country gather together to one place, and the memoirs of the apostles or the writings of the prophets are read, as long as time permits; then, when the reader has ceased, the president verbally instructs, and exhorts to the imitation of these good things. Then we all rise together and pray, and, as we before said, when our prayer is ended, bread and wine and water are brought, and the president in like manner offers prayers and thanksgivings, according to his ability, and the people assent, saying Amen; and there is a distribution to each, and a participation of that over which thanks have been given, and to those who are absent a portion is sent by the deacons. And they who are well to do, and willing, give what each thinks fit; and what is collected is deposited with the president, who helps the orphans and widows and those who, through sickness or any other cause, are in want, and those who are in bonds and the strangers sojourning among us, and in a word takes care of all who are in need.[5]

Several comments are in order to explain what is going on in this passage. By "memoirs of the apostles" Justin means the Gospels and perhaps the letters of Paul.[6] The "writings of the prophets" is his term for the "Old Testament." The "president" is the leader (i.e. "bishop" or "elder") who "presides" over the congregation at worship and prayer. The president is the one who "preaches" which Justin describes as "instruction" or "exhortation" based on the scripture readings. Following the preaching, the congregation stands to pray, after which they greet one another with a kiss.[7] The water that is brought forward with the bread and wine is used to dilute the wine before it is served—a common practice in the ancient world.

We may also notice that the presider offers the prayer "to the best of his ability" which probably means extemporaneously. Yet this does not mean that the presider composed the prayer in some ad hoc fashion, for in another place, Justin tells us that at the Lord's Supper, the presider gives thanks to God "for having created the world, with all the things in it for the sake of humankind, and for delivering us from the evil in which we were [born], and for utterly overthrowing the principalities and powers by Him who suffered according to His will."[8] Thus while the presider probably did not read a prayer out of a book, neither did he or she simply make it up out of thin air. Moreover, this prayer was not really the prayer of the presider alone, since Justin makes a point of saying that the congregation responds with "Amen," which means "so be it." In other words, the congregation has to agree with what the leader prays on their behalf.

The basic shape of the service is Word and Table. We hear the Word of God, and we respond with the "Lord's Supper" which Justin calls "Eucharist" after the Greek word for "thanksgiving." This "Eucharist" is not just ordinary food, as Justin tells us:

> "For not as common bread and common drink do we receive these; but in like manner as Jesus Christ our Savior, having been made flesh by the Word of God, had both flesh and blood for our salvation, so likewise have

we been taught that the food which is blessed by the prayer of His word, and from which our blood and flesh by transmutation are nourished, is the flesh and blood of that Jesus who was made flesh."[9]

While it is not entirely clear what Justin means, this passage suggests that for him the Eucharist was not merely a spiritual object lesson; rather, it involved flesh and blood, both Jesus' and ours. The Christian Lord's Supper is essentially the ongoing process of the Word made flesh, or we might say, the church receiving its identity as the Body of Christ. The order of service that we find in the writings of Justin Martyr, therefore, in basic outline is as follows:

Gathering
Reading the Old Testament and the New Testament
(memoirs of the Apostles)
Sermon (exhortation)
Congregational intercessory prayer
Kiss of Peace
The presentation of the elements used for the Lord's Supper
The "Great Thanksgiving"
Distribution of the bread and wine
(to those present and taken out to those who are absent).

This order of worship described by Justin in the middle of the second century became virtually the universal shape of the liturgy that remained intact for much of Christian history. If it seems familiar to some of us, this is because the "Order of Sunday Worship" found in *The United Methodist Hymnal* (p.3) follows this exact basic shape. The order contains everything that is essential to authentic Christian worship: hearing the Word and responding with our lives; offering our gifts and giving thanks for God's gifts; acknowledging our hunger and being fed; gathering for worship and sending forth for service.

The last point is important, for Justin describes the "eucharistic" worship of the church as literally spilling out into the world to those Christians who cannot be present at the assembly, and to the widows, orphans, the sick and sojourners. This is an order of worship for a church becoming the Body of

Christ in the world. It is why the early church considered the celebration of the Lord's Supper, which they usually referred to as the Eucharist ("thanksgiving"), to be an essential part of weekly Christian worship. In the Eucharist, we receive the Body of Christ in order to become the Body of Christ, bringing into the present situation a concrete, visible manifestation of the Kingdom of God, which is coming into the world. In other words, in its worship, through Word and Table, the church both receives and begins to live out its identity and mission.

Methodist theologian Geoffrey Wainwright has shown how this understanding of worship as the means through which the church found its identity and mission especially through the Eucharist, was a dominant theme in the early church.[10] Wainwright calls this understanding of worship "eschatological," which means it makes present God's ultimate purposes for the world, the coming Kingdom of God.[11] As Wainwright points out, the Eucharist enables Christians to overcome any artificial division between the spiritual and the physical, or the religious and the ethical, the earthly and the heavenly, since through the Lord's Supper Christ is present in bread and wine and in the community gathered around the table.[12]

We could point out many examples of this understanding of worship in the early church, such as this quotation from a fourth-century sermon by John Chrysostom on a text from the Letter to the Hebrews:

> What are the heavenly things he [the author of Hebrews] speaks of here? The spiritual things. For although they are done on earth, yet nevertheless they are worthy of the Heavens. For when our Lord Jesus Christ lies slain [as a sacrifice], when the Spirit is with us, when He who sits at the right hand of the Father is here, when children are made by the Washing [that is baptism], when they are fellow-citizens of those in Heaven, when we have a country, and a city, and citizenship there, when we are foreigners to things here, how can all these be other than "heavenly things"? ... Is not the altar also heavenly? ... How again can the rites which we celebrate be other than heavenly?[13]

As a preacher, John Chrysostom is very direct: the Christian altar and worship (rites) are heavenly things for people who are citizens of God's heavenly country and city. The result of this is not for us to keep our head in the clouds, but to manifest "heaven" here below. Furthermore, our worship joins us to all our fellow citizens of God's Kingdom; that is, other Christians and the angels in heaven who live in fellowship with God. As our United Methodist Great Thanksgiving says, "we join in their unending hymn..." In short, Christian worship, Word and Table, aims to build the Body of Christ for the Kingdom of God in the here and now.

Worship among the Early Methodists

In various ways over the course of the centuries, the church became much less aware of itself as the presence of the eschatological Kingdom of God in history, and more aware of itself as a dominant culture in Europe. There were diverse renewal movements that tried to reclaim the church as making visible the Kingdom of God — St. Francis of Assisi, the Waldensians, the Anabaptists, to name a few — though these movements were less intentionally based in the Eucharist. When we move more than a thousand years ahead in church history to the Methodist movement of John and Charles Wesley in England, we find a renewed emphasis on the Lord's Supper as a "foretaste" of the "heavenly banquet."

Contemporary Methodists may not be aware of how much emphasis John and Charles Wesley put on the Lord's Supper. John Wesley records in his Journals that he took the Lord's Supper on average more than one and a half times per week. For him, the Lord's Supper is one of the chief "means of grace" that God has promised to Christians as channels of divine blessing.[14] Early in his ministry, John wrote a sermon entitled "On the Duty of Constant Communion," reissued later in his life, in which he lays out his reasons for advocating that Christians receive the Lord's Supper as often as possible:

> The grace of God given herein confirms to us the pardon of our sins and enables us to leave them. As our bodies are strengthened by bread and wine, so are our souls by these tokens of the body and the blood of Christ. This is the food of our souls: This gives strength to perform our duty, and leads us on to perfection. If, therefore, we have any regard for the plain command of Christ... then we should neglect no opportunity of receiving the Lord's Supper...[15]

For John Wesley, the Lord's Supper is a means of receiving the power to go on to perfection, which is the goal, the "eschaton" of the Christian life. Later in the sermon, he answers all of the standard arguments against a frequent celebration of the Lord's Supper. For example, to those who say that taking the Lord's Supper frequently makes them feel less reverence for the sacrament, Wesley counters: "Suppose it did; has God ever told you, that when obeying of his command abates your reverence to it, then you may disobey it?" In other words, "God said to do it, so we must do it!" God graciously commands that we do what is good for us whether we feel it or not.

The Wesleys' focus on the Lord's Supper was quite radical, since most Anglican parishes in England celebrated the Lord's Supper only a few times a year. Furthermore, John emphasized the social ministry of the church's worship as outreach to the poor, and saw the Lord's Supper as a "converting ordinance" for the urban masses. Against the practices of the church of his day, both of the Wesleys stressed the importance of singing hymns in worship set to popular tunes. Charles composed a great number of hymns specifically on the Lord's Supper, as well as on the general theme of Christian worship.[16] If John advocated "Constant Communion" in his sermon, Charles emphasized a theme of "constant worship" in his hymns:

> Thee we would be always blessing,
> Serve Thee as thy hosts above,
> Pray and praise thee without ceasing,
> Glory in thy perfect love.[17]

We might hear echoes here, not only of Paul's affirmation to "pray without ceasing" (1 Thessalonians 5:17), but also of Revelation's worshiping hosts of heaven. This hymn concludes with a powerful affirmation that God's salvation will be actually made present in this world through worship:

> Finish, then, Thy new creation
> Pure and spotless let us be
> Let us see Thy great salvation
> Perfectly restored in Thee.
> Changed from glory into glory
> Till in heaven we take our place
> Till we cast our crowns before Thee
> Lost in wonder, love and praise. [18]

This is the eschatological hope of the Christian life, the New Creation, by which we "anticipate our heaven below" as Wesley says in yet another hymn.[19]

The Methodist movement of John and Charles Wesley did truly attempt to manifest the "New Creation" through various ministries of charity: opening orphanages, organizing among the poor, establishing medical facilities, working against the slave trade, among other things. Often John Wesley, the leader of the movement, is cast as a pragmatist who embraced radical new methods of evangelism, such as open-air preaching revivals, to get his message to the poor. Yet Wesley did not see the field preaching events as the main work of the Methodist movement, and very few actual conversions are attributed to such events. Rather, the genius of the Methodist movement was the organization of highly disciplined "societies" which were further divided into classes. The early Methodists took seriously the belief that the church was meant to be the visible body on earth, a community of persons who were "anticipating heaven" and conforming their lives to the worship of heaven as they lived in the world below. These early Methodist societies were far more socially counter-cultural than later Methodism would become, either in England or in the United States.

In 1784 after the Revolutionary War, John Wesley finally agreed to take the extraordinary measure of ordaining his own ministers so that the Methodists in the American colonies could have the sacraments. He sent to the American Methodists *The Sunday Service*, an adaptation of the Anglican *Book of Common Prayer*, slightly shortened in order to make the weekly celebration of the Lord's Supper a practical option for Methodists in the colonies. However, Methodism had already taken root in the colonies without a deep understanding of the Wesleys' eucharistic piety, and a year after John's death in 1791, the American Methodists shortened the ritual considerably. In some ways, the Lord's Supper was supplanted by the Love Feast, a non-sacramental fellowship ritual during which participants shared testimonies of God's work in their lives while they distributed bread and water. But even this sacrament-like service became less and less frequent as the Methodists in the United States gradually gave up the notion of class meetings and disciplined rules in favor of the spontaneous revival and more accessible Sunday school.

AMERICAN METHODIST WORSHIP IN THE 19TH CENTURY

Few Christians have had a greater impact on the history of the English speaking church than the nineteenth century revivalist, Charles G. Finney. Finney did not invent the concept of "revival." The American British colonies in the eighteenth century had seen a great revival, known today as the First Great Awakening, which claimed as a leader the great theologian Jonathan Edwards. The Methodist George Whitefield, who introduced John Wesley to field preaching, also led numerous revival meetings in the colonies. Furthermore, around the year 1800, camp meetings began to spring up along the frontier, where hundreds and sometimes thousands gathered for an extended period of camping and outdoor preaching. Yet Charles Finney is the one who perfected the form of the revival that took hold in the nineteenth century, and continues to influence church life in the United States until the present day.

What Finney added to the revival was a strong dose of practicality together with a heaping of capitalistic advertising. He was a lawyer by training, and he approached the business of revivals like a lawyer who will stop at nothing to win a case. In 1835, Finney gave a series of lectures at Yale University, which were later published under the title, *Lectures on Revivals of Religion*. In his opening lecture, Finney made a statement that must have been startling to the Yale faculty and students who first heard it:

> [A revival] is not a miracle according to another definition of the term miracle — *something above the powers of nature*. There is nothing in religion beyond the ordinary powers of nature. It consists entirely in the *right exercise* of the powers of nature. It is just that, and nothing else.... It is not a miracle, nor dependent on a miracle, in any sense. It is a purely philosophical result of the right use of the constituted means —as much so as any other effect produced by the application of means.[20]

In Finney's view, religion was the work of human beings, inspired by the Holy Spirit to be sure, but a human work nonetheless. This was quite a new understanding of Christian faith and the conversion of sinners. Finney saw little in the work of revivals that was left to surprise; if a pastor followed his formula, revival would surely come.

For Finney, the goal of Christianity was to produce Christians out of sinners, and better Christians out of luke-warm believers. Furthermore, anything that helped to get the attention of people to make them notice the truth of the Gospel could only hasten this process. Before Finney, Protestant Christians had taken one of two approaches to the form of worship. Lutherans and most Anglicans, for example, believed that the form of worship could be based on the tradition of the church as long as the content of the preaching and prayers was biblically based. Others, such as the radical Puritans, thought that the *form of worship itself* had to be based on scriptural precedent. Finney, on the other hand, did not believe that God mandated any sort of form for church worship, discipline, or organization. He believed that throughout the history of the church, bold Christians seeking to renew the church had always felt free to adopt new measures.

The "New Measures" that Finney promoted may sound old-fashioned to us, but in their day they were new and exciting. Some of these New Measures included setting up prayer meetings and "anxious" meetings for people to prepare for the revival. During the revival, persons who were feeling a strong pull toward conversion could sit on a special "anxious bench" located at the front of the church near the pulpit, so that the preacher could direct the preaching toward them. Finney referred to revival preaching as the "message" since he strongly felt that the word was a communication from the preacher to the congregation. Finney also favored using good music with professional song leaders and instrumentalists since these, too, could enhance communication. The pay-off for the revival came with the "altar call" or "harvest," when those seeking conversion could come forward to kneel at the front of the church (for Methodists, this meant the communion rail) to have pastors or other congregational leaders pray them into the Kingdom.

The revival was often an emotionally intense experience, and Finney believed that a regular emotional breakdown in prayerful conversion was good even for the souls of long-standing Christians, since this kept them enthusiastic for their faith. Yet, at the heart of the revival was not merely emotion, but a strong desire for changed lives. Finneyite revivalists became leaders in several of the most important social movements of the nineteenth century: abolition, temperance, and women's right to vote. As Frank Senn has noted, Finney's revival movement combined the practical, no-nonsense philosophical concerns of the nineteenth century rationalists with the warm-hearted emotional populism of the frontier.[21] Finney also was the first explicitly to separate the means for promoting revivals from the substance of the faith. Just as a good sales clerk could sell anything, so could churches be bold in promoting revivals, using whatever produced the desired results.

Finney was very clear about the purpose of the Christian faith: to save souls. He was not particularly concerned about the church as the Body of Christ. Indeed, his vision of the faith was very individualistic and non-sacramental. In his considerable writings on theology and revivalism, one searches in vain for a reference to the Lord's Supper. Since the typical communion service in Finney's day was introspective and penitential, one might wonder if he thought it to be incompatible with a rousing revival service.

Finney's approach to revivals was extremely popular among nineteenth century Methodists, so much so that the style of the revival came to be the standard shape of the regular Sunday service. The contemporary evangelist Billy Graham is the best-known modern proponent of the revival, and his televised "Crusades" use Finney's revival pattern. However, by the mid-century another movement began to have an impact on Methodist worship: the Sunday school. Christian education has played such an important role in contemporary United Methodist church life that it may seem strange to realize that the Sunday school did not really exist before the 1800's. Yet by the 1860s, the Sunday school was a worldwide ecumenical movement that provided such resources as the International Uniform Lesson curriculum, which is still used in many Protestant churches.

While the method of the revival was to move the heart to produce commitment, the goal of the Sunday school was to educate the mind to the same result. Revivals were, typically, led by professional evangelists and song leaders (from other towns, usually, to add to the novelty). The Sunday schools were led by the laity who provided the classroom teachers and the Sunday school superintendents, secretaries, and other officiating roles. This model worked extremely well with the Methodists, who already had a pattern of class meetings led by laity. In the large frontier regions of the United States, where Methodist clergy were scarce, the Sunday school provided structure for weekly meetings that did not require a professional minister of any sort.

Sunday school worship took the form of an assembly. Children gathered under the direction of a superintendent, with an energetic song such as "He Lives, He Lives, Christ Jesus lives today." However, as one might expect, the assembly quickly became more like an informal business meeting with roll calls, announcements, collection of money, and organization of the classes. Awards were handed out for those who attended regularly (how many of us still have "year" pins?), and newcomers received their welcome. The class meetings themselves took place following the "opening exercises." Following the class meetings, the assembly was reconvened with more music, occasionally with presentations by the various classes. The assembly might recite the memory verse of the day, or someone might recite a poem related to the special theme of the day, such as "Mothers' Day" or "Flag Sunday."

The goal of the Sunday school was similar to the revival: conversion. However, there was a difference. The revival aimed at converting people through an emotional response; the Sunday school aimed at converting primarily children through learning and doing. The revival cast a spell; the Sunday school taught a lesson.

The Sunday school was just as oriented toward novel means to accomplish its goals as was the revival. However, the Sunday school was somewhat less oriented toward entertainment (in the nineteenth century no one thought school was supposed to entertain children all the time), and more toward rote memorization and hands-on learning ("Mary, read this chapter in the Bible, please"). This didactic approach to the Christian life was carried over into worship. For the Sunday school movement, the Lord's Supper was not about mystical union with the body of Christ, but an object lesson about Jesus' sacrifice on the cross. Thus like the Revival, the Sunday school was very individualistic in its approach to worship. There was little understanding of the universal Body of Christ made present in the worshiping assembly.

The revival mined the emotional energy of the American frontier can-do spirit, and the Sunday school tapped into the American practical desire for personal discipline and advancement. However, as Methodists, United Brethren, and Evangelicals began to be prominent in the various towns and cities of the young republic, they also began to return to the liturgical roots of the *Book of Common Prayer* and the Anglican Church as a model of how to be a respectable church. In the 1820's, Nathan Bangs scandalized the Methodists of New York by committing the wasteful extravagance of laying down carpet in the chancel area of his church. By the turn of the century, Methodists were building churches with pointed arches, stained-glass windows and pipe organs. Moreover, the church began, gradually, to incorporate some Anglican styles of liturgy: robed choirs, candles on the communion table and the use of printed prayers. The first Methodist hymnal to contain a printed order of worship appeared in 1905; this order included more liturgical ceremony and prayer than the simple orders published at the beginning of the nineteenth century. [22] As the denomination began to shed some of its frontier coarseness, a growing concern for dignity in worship coincided with Methodism's growing class-consciousness and its deepening sense of civic purpose as a moral leader of the American nation. For, while the U.S. Constitution had avoided conscripting a church to be the state religion, the Methodists volunteered for the job.

All of these influences (the Wesleys, the Revival, the Sunday school, and civil religion) have melded into a complex understanding of worship for Methodists in the twenty-first century. In addition to these movements, we find a greatly increased awareness of the complex relation of worship to ethnicity and gender. African-American and Asian-American churches typically adopt worship forms quite different from each other, and both of these differ from the typical middle-class white suburban congregation. Nevertheless, there has been a tremendous and fruitful cross-fertilization of worship styles among the various ethnic traditions. Likewise, the growing leadership of women in ministry and theology has led to increased awareness of the male-dominated tone of some "traditional" liturgical language and ritual. Today, few congregations could sing "Rise Up, O Men of God" without becoming self-consciously aware that at least half of the congregation is female.[23] Furthermore, many United Methodists find the use of the image of God as Father to be stifling unless it is expanded with images of God as Mother, or with gender-neutral language of God as "loving" or "Creator" or "Source of Life".

United Methodists have become increasingly aware that not only ethnicity and gender, but other diverse factors as social class, age, physical ability, geographic region, and even size of congregation influence worship styles and content. Indeed, if there were one consistent overarching principle that characterizes United Methodist worship in the early twenty-first century, it would be "diversity."

While diversity is a sign of health, it also can become a problem, for diversity *per se* cannot hold a people together within congregations, much less across a denomination. Thus, there has been, in recent years, an increased longing for something that ties us together and gives meaning to our lives as community.[24] One of the most striking responses to the longing for community has been the rise of "megachurches," those congregations with thousands of worshipers gathering each week to praise God, hear well-performed music, and receive an inspiring, biblically-based message. Indeed, central to the success of megachurches is their ability to manifest this feeling of comprehensive community—thousands worshiping together can create a sense of transcendent togetherness.

Most congregations will not have the sheer numbers to do this on their own. Most United Methodists will need something else, something that helps them see beyond their local congregations, something like the service that Justin Martyr describes, something that lets them pray, *and so with your people on earth and all the company of heaven, we praise your name, and join their unending hymn.*

What we need, finally, is a spiritually transcendent, historically grounded, thoroughly biblical, potentially transformative, religiously comprehensive *liturgy.* We suggest we already have just such a liturgy in our *United Methodist Hymnal* and *Book of Worship.* What we need to do is to learn how to use this liturgy for the glory of God and the transformation of our churches.

Endnotes

1 William W. How, "For All The Saints," *UMH* 711.
2 See *UMH* p. 9.
3 This treatise is called an "apology," which is an explanation of the faith to outsiders.
4 *First Apology* 65. The translation of Justin is adapted from A. Roberts and J. Donaldson, eds, *The Ante-Nicene Fathers*, Vol. 1., (Peabody, MA: Hendrickson Publishers, Inc., 1995) 159 ff.
5 *First Apology* 67.
6 The term "New Testament" was not used as a title for the collection of Christian writings in middle of the second century.
7 The Apostle Paul mentions the holy kiss four times in his letters: Romans 16:16, 1 Corinthians 16:20; 2 Corinthians 13:12; I Thessalonians 5:26. The kiss is also mentioned in 1 Peter 5:14.
8 Justin Martyr, *Dialogue with Trypho* 41.
9 *First Apology* 66.
10 Geoffrey Wainwright, *Eucharist and Eschatology* (Akron, Ohio: OSL Publications, 2002).
11 Eschatology comes from the Greek worship *eschaton*, which means "end," as in "the end times."
12 For an excellent and moving treatment of the importance of the church as the Body of Christ centered in the Eucharist, see William T. Cavanaugh, *Torture and Eucharist: Theology, Politics, and the Body of Christ* (Malden, MA: Blackwell Pub., 1999) 203-233,
13 *Homilies on Hebrews* XIV.3, from *Nicene and Post-Nicene Fathers*, ed. Philip Schaff, First Series, Vol. 14, (Peabody, MA: Hendrickson Publishers, Inc., 1995), translation altered by W. Cavanaugh, *Torture and Eucharist* 224.
14 See his sermon, "The Means of Grace" (Wesley Sermon 16).
15 "The Duty of Constant Communion" (Wesley Sermon 101, I.3)
16 See J. Ernest Rattenbury, *The Eucharistic Hymns of John and Charles Wesley* (Akron, Ohio: OSL Publications, 1996).
17 "Love Divine all Loves excelling," stanza 3, *UMH 384*.
18 "Love Divine," stanza 4.
19 "O For a Thousand Tongues to Sing" stanza 7, *UMH* 57.
20 Charles G. Finney, *Lectures on Revivals of Religion* (Cambridge, MA: Harvard University Press, 1960), 12-13.
21 Frank C. Senn, *Christian Liturgy, Catholic and Evangelical* (Minneapolis: Fortress Press, 1997) 563-4.

[22] Before the 1964 *Book of Worship*, Methodist rituals and orders of service were published in the *Discipline*; orders of service did not regularly appear in hymnals until the twentieth century.

[23] Although the *UMH* includes this hymn (576), it suggests substituting "Ye Saints" for "O Men."

[24] In a feature story for the on-line journal *Religion News* (August 10, 1999), Scott Thumma, a researcher for Hartford Seminary points out that many of those in Generation X find themselves longing for traditional ritual, rather than entertainment evangelism. We might note here the recent, unexpected success of a recording of Gregorian chant.

Chapter 4

Finish, Then, Thy New Creation

O God, the Holy Spirit,
come to us, and among us;
come as the wind, and cleanse us;
come as the fire, and burn;
come as the dew, and refresh;
convict, convert, and consecrate
many hearts and lives
to our great good and to thy greater glory;
and this we ask for Jesus Christ's sake. Amen.[1]

Hardly a week goes by without the average pastor receiving an article, book advertisement, or workshop invitation from experts offering new ways to be more creative, contemporary or relevant in worship. "Adopt this model, change this pattern, drop this dead practice," much of the worship renewal literature tells us, "in order to make your worship more alive and vital."[2] Diversity and change were the hallmarks of United Methodist worship in the late twentieth century, and this continues to be the case for worship in the twenty-first century. The tremendous changes we have seen in practices have taught us a great deal about the importance of honoring the various differences among us—gender, ethnicity, age, and ability, to name a few. Yet there are some in our congregations who are frustrated and worn out by changes that seem arbitrary, or that offer a shallow approach to the various differences among us by treating these differences as matters of personal taste. After all, why should they invest themselves in worship if it changes at the whim of different worship leaders or pastors? Some churches may feel pressed to become something they are not, and lose their own sense of being part of the family of Christ. Many of our congregations suffer from what we call "liturgical whiplash" because they feel frustrated by so much radical and contradictory change. If worship is something to which we give our hearts in order to unite with the universal praise of the saints, then it needs to have the sort of stability that allows worshipers to trust it.

Proponents of worship renewal typically rely on the latest sociological surveys or demographic predictions about the "Baby-boomers," "Generation X," or "Ethnic communities" to predict the future of the church. Since our work is about worship renewal in the emerging church, we want to fulfill the expectations of our readers by saying with *absolute confidence* that we *know what the future of Christian worship will look like*:

> "Then I saw a new heaven and a new earth…And I heard a loud voice from the throne saying, 'See, the home of God is among mortals…' I saw no temple in the city, for its temple is the Lord God the Almighty and the Lamb. And the city has no need of sun or moon to shine on it, for the glory of God is its light…"[3]

Because the future of our worship entails God's new heaven and earth, any renewal must anticipate this eschatological vision whenever we gather to worship the God of Jesus Christ in the power of the Holy Spirit. While it may be helpful to be aware of the social trends in our surrounding culture, the church needs to see itself as an alternative community that God can use to influence cultural trends, or even to resist some aspects of our host culture. We anticipate our future by how we worship in the present.

As we move toward this future God has in store for us, we believe that this new millenium will be the time for a different understanding of "megachurch." The modern term "megachurch" designates a single congregation with ten thousand members or more. Frankly, that is much too small to manifest the church God intends for the future. For again, as John of Patmos tells us: "After this I looked, and there was a great multitude that no one could count, from every nation from all tribes and peoples and languages, standing before the throne and before the Lamb...they are before the throne of God, and worship God day and night..." (Revelation 7:9, 15). Therefore, we believe that what the church needs now is a liturgy for a "mega-mega-church" that transcends individual congregations small and large, uniting our hearts in the universal praise of God, transforming us into the visible body of Christ. This will require an approach to worship that emphasizes both the local congregation and the universal, or to use traditional language, "catholic" church, and that honors diversity while striving for unity.

It is important, therefore, that worship planners understand some fundamental principles by which liturgy operates and how they might utilize these principles.

PRINCIPLES GOVERNING THE WAY LITURGIES "WORK"

The "liturgy" is the order of words (printed, sung, spoken or otherwise) and actions (gestures, movement) which congregations use for their worship. While it is theoretically possible for *individuals* to worship without ritual (the rare mystical experience or vision, for example), it is practically impossible for *communities* to worship without liturgy. Furthermore as we note in chapter one, liturgy is fundamentally ritual. Ritual has certain characteristics that suggest some basic principles for how liturgy as ritual "works." The anthropologist Roy Rappaport has outlined several characteristics of ritual that provide some very practical evaluation tools for worship planners.[4]

1. *Liturgy is handed down to us.* Or, as Rappaport states the principle, ritual is "canonical." We do not "make up" the words and actions of our rituals from scratch, nor do we control their fundamental meaning; rather, they come to us through tradition. In that regard, liturgy is very much like the canon of scripture, which we also receive through our tradition. We contemporary Christian do not "make up" the Bible. On the contrary, accepting the Bible as the privileged witness to the Word of God is an essential feature of what "makes us" the church! In the same way, we do not have to invent the Lord's Supper; we receive it as our tradition going back to Jesus' actions at the Last Supper. When we have new persons to bring into the church, we don't have to wonder, "Gee, how can we do that?" We have the tradition of baptism that goes back to the beginning of the church. This does not mean that changes or additions to our liturgy of the Lord's Supper and Baptism do not occur. Indeed, the brief historical overview in chapter three shows that the actual liturgical practices of Eucharist and Baptism have changed over the years. Nevertheless, there are limits to how much a ritual can be changed and still be received by a community as a ritual. (Just try changing an established holiday tradition with children and you will see what we mean!) For, in the history of the church (at least until fairly recently) when churches sought to change a ritual practice, it was not in order to make this practice more interesting, or more relevant to the present, but to make the practice more clearly connected to its origin in the tradition.

Clearly, understanding this "traditional" feature of liturgy, does not mean that change does not happen or need to happen. But, it does suggest that leaders should take great care to connect all changes to Christian tradition and teach this to our congregations. For example, the fairly recent United Methodist practice of remembering one's baptism has become a powerful rededication liturgy for many congregations. Yet, for congregations to understand that a pastor flinging water from her fingertips did not constitute a "re-baptism" of those seated in the pews, we know that pastors had to explain, through preaching or by some other means, just what was going on in this strange and new (to United Methodists, anyway) ritual. Baptismal renewal has to be placed clearly with the tradition of Baptism in order for it to do what it is supposed to do.

Beside the official Ritual, there is a place for more spontaneous rituals or for rituals that address occasional, but genuine needs in our churches. We have participated in a variety of new liturgies, such as a service for the loss of a stillborn baby, a mass for the celebration and protection of the earth, and a retirement liturgy. However, just because something is done once and works well in that context does not mean it has to become the "first annual…." Likewise, just because our St. Francis "Blessing of the Animals" promises to grow as a family service does not mean we should open weekly worship to our pets. In short, innovative practices will have their place alongside our regular worship, but not as a replacement for it. If such liturgical practices withstand the test of time, the future church will see them emerge as normative.

Once a ritual has become firmly embedded in the tradition, its actual source is forgotten unless it originates with some very important historical figure.[5] So, for example, while we recognize that the Lord's Supper is instituted by Jesus, no one knows who first began Eucharistic prayers with "The Lord be with you." We know that something like the Apostles' Creed existed since at least the late 2nd century A.D., but no one knows who actually began to use such a creed in connection with baptism. A more recent example is the widely-used call and response, "God is good/ All the time/All the time/God is good." Congregations who use this response are completely uninterested in the author. What matters is that the congregation knows it from memory.

Obviously, services of Christian worship will contain much that can be attributed to a source. For example, our hymnbooks will give composers of tunes and authors of hymn texts. Modern copyright laws require us to display the source of the musical resources we might print in a bulletin. The same holds true for a prayer text or other liturgical material that comes from a published source. Nevertheless, respect for copyright law notwithstanding, such "named" sources can only effectively function as Christian liturgy when they are set within an overall ritual that is received from our Christian tradition, even though understandings of "Christian tradition" may differ greatly depending upon denominational and congregational histories. Worship leaders that respect the principle of canonicity will be careful not to overwhelm a congregation with unfamiliar, newer "resources" that come from outside the tradition of the congregation.

2. *Liturgy has structure or form.* This is how we recognize something as liturgy and not some other type of behavior. To say that ritual has a structure does not mean that it ought to be "formal" in the sense of "stuffy, " but that it has structure within which spontaneity can occur. Furthermore, as Rappaport points out, structure does not mean that ritual avoids all novelty. Sermons, for example, might vary greatly over the course of weeks. The preacher could preach from behind the pulpit or in front of it. The sermon could include an object lesson or a song or a dramatic reading. None of these novelties alter the overall order of worship.

Genuine spontaneity, moreover, can be powerful. We recall the baptism of an infant that cried throughout the ceremony. After the water was poured over the child's head, the pastor remarked, "You should cry, little one: it is an awesome and difficult thing to receive the promises of God." This spontaneous remark was a starling moment of ritual power for that congregation. But this does not mean that those exact words should be repeated the next time a baby is received in baptism. Spontaneity, by definition, cannot be staged or coerced.

Worship leaders who understand the structure of liturgy will not promote novelty for novelty's sake. In talking with a pastor about the varied order of worship in his church, he said, "I like to keep 'em guessing!" We suspect the pastor takes this approach to avoid the complacency of rote repetition. However, "enforced" spontaneity is really a form of manipulation that will make worshipers feel disconnected from their worship.

On the other hand, liturgy should never be dull. We suggest that our liturgy should be *lavish* rather than *austere*. To illustrate, for baptisms we should use an abundant amount of water that can be seen and heard as it is poured into the font. The standard joke is that most Methodist baptisms could pass for dry cleaning. While we recognize that baptism by sprinkling is a valid baptism, why should we take such a minimalist approach to this important life-changing event? United Methodists can reclaim the practices of immersion and pouring, even for the baptism of infants.[6] We can think of numerous examples where dullness can drain liturgy of its vitality: the use of pre-broken crackers for the Lord's Supper; psalms read by a leader on auto-pilot; the Lord's Prayer spoken as if no one is listening. We reckon that the "stuffiness" people often attribute to liturgy is really a reaction to liturgy that is poorly done, rather than to the form of the liturgy itself.

When appropriately employed, liturgical structure provides a shape for our joyous prayer and praise to God and for our interactions with our fellow worshipers (the boisterous sharing of the sign of peace in some congregations comes to mind). In this sense, form is to worship as structure is to music. Structure is what distinguishes music from noise. Worship planners should recognize that the structure of liturgy is what turns a crowd into the body of Christ.

3. *Liturgy is conservative.* Liturgy is resistant to change, or, as Rappaport notes, ritual is invariant, more or less. Rappaport says "more or less" because absolute invariability is neither desirable nor even possible. People will vary how they stand, or sit, or make certain kinds of motions such as bowing, swaying or kneeling—and gradually congregations change how these things fit into their worship. But, overall, worship tends to conserve the previous patterns rather than embracing new patterns.

Furthermore, this conservative aspect of liturgy means that it is generally easier to add something than to take something out or radically change something that is already in place. Orders of worship have grown as children's sermons, praise choruses, passing the peace and other liturgical acts have been added over the course of years. In some ways, the order of worship is like an attic into which more and more gets stuffed until finally we have to do a cleaning.

There are limits to how much an order of worship can hold. When the service regularly goes unnecessarily long, people complain, and components are dropped. This can present some difficulty for worship planners. We know of one church that began singing a song to remember people on their birthdays and dropped a reading of scripture in order to make room for the new ceremony. We should question whether it is a good practice for Christians, who claim baptism as our "new birth," to honor "birthdays" by omitting the reading of scripture. *Worship leaders who understand the conservative nature of liturgy will take care to preserve the essential patterns so that what gets dropped will not be something integral to the order of worship.*

Because liturgy is conservative, changes must be introduced slowly in order for the congregation to accept them. Even the suggestions we offer in this book, such as the weekly use of the service of Word and Table, should be introduced gradually. A congregation that is used to the revival pattern may balk at replacing the "Invitation to Christian Discipleship" with a weekly celebration of the Lord's Supper, *unless* they can see that the invitation to the Lord's Table *is* an invitation to discipleship. Similarly, a congregation is more likely to accept a new, central and more visible location for the communion table if the worship leaders explain the change before hand, rather than having people be surprised by all the re-arranged furniture some Sunday morning. At one church he served, Ed had some success in introducing this particular change in worship by first bringing up the issue in an adult Sunday School class. He noted that many churches place their communion table in a central location so that the pastor can stand behind it during the Lord's Supper. He also proposed that this arrangement symbolizes Christ present in the midst of the family of God. On the following communion Sunday, he arrived to find several leaders of the congregation moving the communion table away from the wall. One commented, "We liked your suggestion. Is this enough room for you to stand here behind the table?" While we may not be able to make every needed change so painlessly, *worship leaders will strive to enable changes in worship to come from the congregation, rather than enforcing them "from the top."*

On a practical level, the conservative nature of ritual means that *worship leaders need to be very cautious about introducing new rituals.* We are tempted to suggest that worship leaders should not introduce a new ritual that they do not intend for the congregation to continue until Jesus returns! For once it becomes established, congregation may even want to continue repeating a ritual of dubious value (such as baptizing babies with rosebuds) merely because a former pastor thought it was "meaningful."

4. *Liturgy is essentially performance.* What we have in a book or on a printed page, or even in our rote memory is not really liturgy until it is done. As the "work of the people," liturgy must be acted out.

Some might feel uncomfortable with referring to liturgy as a performance because this sounds as if we are saying that worship is like the theater. Indeed, the philosopher Kierkegaard makes this explicit comparison—worship *is* like the theater. He notes that just as the theater requires an actor, a prompter (to help with the lines), and an audience, so also worship has an actor, a prompter and an audience. Kierkegaard points out that most of us act as if the preacher is the actor, and God, the Holy Spirit is the prompter, and the congregation is the audience. Rather, he says, the congregation is the actor in worship, performing their prayer and praise before God; the minister is the prompter, helping them with their lines; God is the audience.

We might quibble with this comparison, for surely God also "acts" in our worship. Nevertheless, the comparison contains something profound: the whole congregation performs the liturgy, not merely the pastors up front. *Worship planners must recognize that the congregation is not the audience; they are the performers.*

Yet the congregation does not have to read or sing everything aloud together. Instead, it is better to understand and plan worship as an interplay of different roles. The congregation, for example, will need to play its role of offering regular assent to what is being said. African-American churches and some white southern churches use the word "Amen" to punctuate prayers, songs, and exhortations by various leaders, turning even the sermon into a group participation act. But, even without such vocal participation, congregations must understand the indispensable ministry they perform in worship. Participation in liturgy is the group participation of a ball team or a symphony orchestra. Or, as St. Paul states, "For just as the body is one and has many members, and all the members of the body, though many, are one body, so it is with Christ" (I Corinthians 12:12). Preachers will preach, song leaders will lead songs, ushers will direct, and readers will read the lessons while the whole congregation will listen, sing, respond, pray, and always offer their spoken (or silent) "amen." *Worship planners should think of ways to promote distinctive ministries of leading to facilitate diversity and cooperation in worship.*

5. *Liturgy is communication.* This action may seem obvious, since, of course, sermons, scripture readings, prayers, etc. are communication. However, what we intend here is that liturgy is communication as *liturgy.* In other words, it makes a real difference that the "sermon" is "preached" in worship; that is what makes it a sermon instead of a lecture or speech. Even those aspects of the liturgy that are not word-oriented (standing, kneeling, eating, drinking) are still essentially communication—they communicate respect, penitence, friendship, or some other attitude.

The "special" aspects of the liturgy are among its most important points of communication. For example, it is important for liturgy to be connected with Sunday. A church that changes the main day of Christian worship from Sunday to midweek, even for good reasons, has fundamentally altered the nature of what is being done in worship. In the tradition of the church, Sunday is the weekly remembrance of the day of Jesus' resurrection, the first day of the week represents the first day of God's New Creation, and it is the "Lord's Day," according to John of Patmos. The recognition of Sunday as the day for the church to worship God connects our worship life to our experience of time in a fundamental relationship. Of course, Christians can gather to worship God any time and place, but this cannot change our recognition of the priority of Sunday. The third commandment, "Remember the Sabbath and keep it holy" reminds us that time is not ours to manipulate according to our own wants and needs.

Liturgy not only communicates obvious meaning, it also communicates deeper levels of meaning that are not obvious, or that may not be fully understandable. As we note in chapter one, rituals communicate meanings that cannot easily be put into words. We can say that eating together makes us a family, but it is very difficult to describe exactly how that happens, or even all that it means. And yet, eating together is a central act of Christian worship.

Worship planners must be aware that liturgy communicates our fundamental Christian identity as the Body of Christ, as much by how we do things as by the words we say. Therefore, we should be very concerned about such things as architectural boundaries to the physically disabled, or about the presence (or absence) of children in our worship, or how the remaining bread and wine are handled after the Lord's Supper. We should never let lack of attention to detail place a barrier in the way of what we intend for our worship to communicate. We may, for example, say, "This is the blood of Christ poured out for you..." but if we use cheap, plastic, disposable cups, it will be difficult for anyone to believe that we truly mean it.

6. *Liturgy is about both the "here and now" and the eternal kingdom of God.*[7] Liturgy forms us into the Body of Christ and connects us to the worship of the host of heaven, but it also involves the present concerns of worshipers in any given congregation. Events that take place in our communities, the nation, or the world will become a part of the prayer and praise of our worship. As we write this, our congregation has been shaken by the murder in our community of a well-known black man by a local white supremacist. Certainly, this tragedy has been lifted up in the preaching and public prayer in our church. We may be aware of individuals who are suffering or who have experienced great joy. We bring adults, children, or infants into our community through baptism, and we see them as *individuals* with distinctive concerns, needs, and gifts for the life of the congregation. That is the stuff of worship in the here and now.

Liturgy must accommodate the church in the particular state of its existence in the "here and now." Liturgies will need to have a significant place for variation—extemporaneous prayer, joyous acclamations and songs, creative sermons—to accommodate the present experience of the congregation. Yet, the liturgy also must have the stability of structure and content to communicate the historically continuous tradition of the church that points the church toward the universal purpose of worship. *Worship leaders and congregations should recognize that all liturgies must have a balance of these dynamics: the contemporary and the traditional, the present and the transcendent.*

HOW SHALL WE WORSHIP?

Let us summarize all that we have been saying. In chapter one, we argue that worship is how God forms us to be witnesses to the truth of Jesus Christ to a world that has become content with "virtual reality." In chapter two, we examine several passages from the New Testament which demonstrate how worship embodies the truth of Jesus Christ in the world and connects our worship to God's New Creation. In chapter three we show how the church has modified and sometimes lost this biblical understanding of worship even while exploring important new aspects of worship. In this chapter we have proposed that liturgy as ritual follows certain rules that must be taken into account as we consider how we plan and conduct our worship.

Our audacious proposal is that the time has come for us to redirect our energy away from experimentation and toward understanding and practicing the official ritual of our United Methodist Church as found in our hymnals, *The United Methodist Hymnal* (1989), *Mil Voces Para Celebrar: Himnario Metodista* (1996), and in *The United Methodist Book of Worship* (1992).

But first, a disclaimer: we do *not* mean that all United Methodist Churches should slavishly limit their music to the hymns in the hymnal or that congregations should only use the prayers exactly as they are printed in *The Book of Worship*. Congregations provide the local context for worship and should supplement the liturgical materials of the *Hymnal* and the *Book of Worship* with songs, prayers, and even some rites that connect to their local traditions. Certainly, we will need to continue our adaptations of our liturgy into the various languages that United Methodists use for worship.

We *are* proposing, however, that the official United Methodist liturgies for A Service of Word and Table, the Baptismal Covenant, Morning and Evening Praise and Prayer, and also the pastoral rites for Christian marriage and for funerals be used as our *essential pattern for liturgy.* The *Discipline* (2004: para 1114.1 for General Church, 629.4b for Annual Conference Board of Discipleship structures) asks us to promote the use of the hymnals and *The Book of Worship* among local churches, and most of our congregations use the official hymnal, if not *The Book of Worship.* However, many of our worship planners treat the sacramental and pastoral rites of our church as "resources" that can be used or not, or modified, or re-written as they want. Consequently, the style and content of worship can vary dramatically from one pastor to another, from one worship leader to the next. Unfortunately, since many worship leaders will not have a sufficiently high level of skill and knowledge for writing prayers or composing orders of service, such changes almost always detract from the liturgical materials as they are written. This may seem harsh, and we do not want to suggest that worship leaders generally lack skills. Of course, worship leaders will need to make changes to adapt the liturgy to the local setting. Nevertheless, we are asserting that the liturgies *as they are written* have been carefully worked out over the course of many years of congregational trials and expert evaluation; they are prayerful and biblical, theologically articulate and historically based.

We suggest that worship leaders focus their creative abilities on implementing and interpreting the United Methodist Ritual, rather than on revising them or writing newer materials. We suspect that some worship planners feel a little guilty if they don't write their own liturgies or look for other creative new materials in the voluminous worship resource literature. We hope that our proposal will relieve pastors and worship planners from feeling that they always have to re-invent the wheel. We *have* a set of liturgical services that we need to use to their full capacity. We do not, however, promote the use of our official Ritual because we think this will make the work of worship planners much easier. Worship planning will always be difficult (though, we hope, joyful) work. We promote the use of our official Ritual because we believe this is the most practical, accessible and faithful way for us to renew worship for the emerging church in this new millennium.

1. *Worship in the emerging church must connect us across congregational and even denominational lines in a global, universal reality.* Worship provides a congruent story on the catholic and denominational levels for congregations to understand how they fit into "the big picture" of God's New Creation. Just as Justin Martyr described a service of "Word and Table" in the early church, so our Ritual contains services of "Word and Table" that follow essentially the same order. This is the basic order followed today by most Christians throughout the world. The twentieth century has seen an amazing convergence in the official rituals of Anglicans, Lutherans, Presbyterians, and Roman Catholics. Thus, our Ritual connects us with the ancient Christian tradition, and it connects us across denominations.

As we noted earlier, the Service of Word and Table joins our praise with God's "people on earth" and "the entire company of heaven." It promotes the reading of scripture, with lessons from the Old Testament and New Testament. And, most importantly, it pre-supposes that the celebration of the Lord's Supper (or the Eucharist or Holy Communion) is the standard *weekly* celebration, just as it was for the first Christians.

We have not said enough about how important we believe the recovery of the regular, weekly practice of the Eucharist will be for the emerging church. For United Methodists, one of the most significant indications of our recovery of the Lord's Supper is the adoption by the 2004 General Conference of *This Holy Mystery: A United Methodist Understanding of Holy Communion* (available for free on the world wide web at http://www.gbod.org/worship/thisholymystery). This official teaching document encourages congregations to embrace weekly celebration of the Lord's Supper on the Lord's Day as the "complete pattern of Christian Worship."

The recovery of weekly communion has been one of the "megatrends" of the twentieth century among both Protestant and Roman Catholic Christians. Along with increased frequency of communion has come a renewed understanding of the Lord's Supper as thanksgiving. For many Protestants, the Lord's Supper had become a very penitential ceremony, which focused mainly on the individual believer's connection to the suffering of Christ.[8] This narrow focus on the suffering is gradually expanding as Christians recovers the Lord's Supper as a joyful celebration of Christ's living presence among us. Along with the recovery of thanksgiving, we are also beginning to reclaim the early Christian belief that the supper makes present the Body of Christ in the community of believers and conveys power for living as the Body of Christ in the world. As stated in *This Holy Mystery,* "The whole assembly actively celebrates Holy Communion. All who are baptized into the body of Christ Jesus become servants and ministers within that body, which is the church." "The one body, drawn together by the one Spirit, is fully realized when all its many parts eat together in love and offer their lives in service at the Table of the Lord."[9] We believe that this trend toward a fuller, richer, and more-frequent celebration of the Eucharist will continue in the emerging church as Christians express their longing for transcendence in worship.

The service of Baptismal Covenant I, in the section entitled "Renunciation of Sin and Profession of Faith" provides a vivid example of the transcendent dimension of Christian life and worship. The pastor asks of the candidates (or the parents or sponsors of small children) three important questions:

> Do you renounce the spiritual forces of wickedness, reject the evil power of this world, and repent of your sin?
> Do you accept the freedom and power God gives you to resist evil, injustice, and oppression in whatever forms they present themselves?

Do you confess Jesus Christ as your Savior, put your
whole trust in his grace, and promise to serve him as
your Lord, in union with the church which Christ has
opened to people of all ages, nations, and races?[10]

These questions are bold points of connection to a massive
ovement of God on earth and in heaven. What will it mean
our churches to live out our renunciation of "the spiritual
ces of wickedness" and "the evil powers of the world"? This
guage reflects a church that seeks to live toward a New
aven and Earth, a church that is connected to the Revelation
ohn of Patmos. Our United Methodist Ritual provides or-
s of worship and sacrament that connect us across
congregations, across denominations, even across nations as the
universal people of God in Jesus Christ.

2. *Worship in the emerging church will focus more on patterns of performance than on printed words.* Since worship is
primarily action, it is important to follow patterns so that people
know how to worship. The United Methodist Ritual promotes
a structured flexibility that gives shape to the service of worship without suppressing the spontaneous expressions of prayer
and thanksgiving and without stifling creativity in music and
preaching. Indeed, structure *allows* for spontaneity more than
lack of structure because it gives the congregation the freedom
to respond in worship without fearing that the service will de-
teriorate into chaos.

An excellent example of the structured flexibility of the *Book
of Worship* is the form of prayer used by Korean United Methodists, *Tongsung Kido*, which means "Pray aloud."[11] In this form
of prayer, the leader of worship announces the time for prayer
and asks the congregation to pray out-loud together *at the same
time.*[12] This type of prayer is noisy, intense, beautiful, and even
musical. Yet, it is only viable for congregations that have a
strong sense of control, or else it can become chaotic.

The order of worship allows for creativity in music, and
our Ritual does not favor any one style. Our *Hymnal* contains a
wide variety of music from different countries and many different time periods. Church music leaders also have the

freedom to supplement the hymnal with musical forms the congregation will appreciate. Much of the literature for church renewal stresses the importance of culturally-authentic, singable music for the vitality of worship. Frankly, some of the contemporary gospel songs can be musically and theologically trite (at a praise service we once heard a man whisper to his wife, "Does being spiritual mean you have to like to sing junk?"). Nevertheless, music will be the most obvious place where the best of popular culture is blended with the liturgical forms of the church.

The placement of the service music in the liturgy probably should be fairly stable. Stability allows us to experience the full effect of variety when it occurs. During the offertory on most Sundays of the year, our church sings the doxology, "Praise God, from Whom All Blessings Flow" in a version which has an abundance of "alleluias."[13] During the season of Lent, we use a doxology that does not contain "alleluia" in order to follow an ancient tradition that withholds this particular word of praise during the Lenten fast. On Easter, when we return to the doxology with the "alleluias," the words ring out like thunder on a sunny day as we praise God for the Resurrection.

The repetition of various parts of worship, such as this doxology, allows people to learn the liturgy "by heart." Generally, we think it best to minimize the amount of reading a congregation must do in order to participate in the service. Most people can easily learn the Lord's Prayer by heart and can pray it aloud with a congregation in worship. It is even possible for individual worshipers to "edit" the prayer even as the whole congregation prays out loud (some of us might be "trespassers," others "debtors," and others "sinners"). However, when someone prints an unfamiliar prayer for the congregation to pray together, the congregation has to read from a text. A little of this goes a long way, and is less conducive to spontaneity and diversity than the use of standard texts.

Repetition of standard liturgical prayers and acclamations by the congregation can become an important feature of congregational identity. This ability to repeat things is especially important for those with limited reading ability and for children. For example, some years ago, Sara's inner city parish had been successful in gathering some neighborhood children for a confirmation class. Prodding the children on what they liked about worship, feeling confident that her folksy sermon style had really drawn them in, she prompted, "Maybe it's my preaching that you like?" To which Deron replied, "Well, that's okay, but we *really* like the "Holy, holy, holy!" Singing that response in the weekly communion ritual connected with ten-year-old Deron as if it were a school cheer. While he may not understand the sermon, learning to sing the "Holy, holy, holy" made him a part of the team. That is what the structured flexibility of our United Methodist Ritual can provide. Responses such as "God is good — all the time" or "The Lord be with you — And also with you" work best when we do not have to read them out of a bulletin. We strongly recommend the use of short responses and choruses with singable tunes, especially those that use biblical passages, which congregations can use frequently enough to know them by heart. This is not really an innovation, since the church has used choruses for centuries. In addition to the acclamations of the Great Thanksgiving ("Holy, holy, holy," "Christ has died," "Amen"), we might consider our familiar doxologies, the *Gloria Patri*, and various benedictions (we grew up singing "God Be With You Till We Meet Again").

Some larger congregations are experimenting with projecting words to hymns and choruses on large screens so that worshipers do not have to keep their faces buried in a book or worship bulletin. This approach may work in churches that have the technological tools to do it well. If it is done poorly (we have seen a few embarrassing attempts at "hi-tech" using old overhead projectors), it will be a major distraction. Overall, however, whether a congregation uses projections, a hymnal, or a bulletin insert, we suggest that congregations not be overwhelmed with too many new, unfamiliar hymns.

The emphasis in the emerging church on patterns of performance will mean worship will come to be understood as an exciting, participatory *event*, rather than as an hour of passive education. While education will certainly take place in worship, this education will come through the *practice* of prayer and praise, shaping through action rather than through didactic preaching. United Methodist Ritual is constructed to engage congregations in precisely this manner, as a dramatic, participatory event.

3. *Worship in the emerging church will be the holistic matrix for every aspect of congregational life.* In pre-modern times, life in general was more connected. Work, family, religion, social life all fit into one whole experience. In the modern world, these aspects of our lives became compartmentalized and separated, ostensibly with the intention of keeping each component of our lives intact. In our emerging post-modern world, we see a trend toward putting things back together. Shopping malls and "super-stores" where one can take care of all sorts of "needs" under one roof represent one aspect of this trend toward reconnecting our lives. Large churches with their total child centers and food courts represent another aspect of this trend, providing a holistic matrix in which family life, the nurture of children, recreation, fellowship, community service all *fit together* in a system connected by evangelism, Christian education, and spiritual formation.

We believe this is a significant trend that the emerging church must address. Nevertheless, one cannot avoid the critique that in many communities the "one roof" discount store has meant the demise of the small town square that promoted community life. Similarly, the megachurch model is likely to intimidate the vast majority of United Methodists, despite the fact that many small churches with their potluck dinners, shared child-care duty, small group interaction and outreach to those in need already model a holistic approach to church life.

Our *United Methodist Book of Worship* provides a holistic framework for all of these aspects of church life. Evangelism is the process of bringing persons to Christ and into the church. Our services of Baptismal Covenant (*UMH* 32-49) provide the door to bring people into the church through baptism, or to reconnect them to the church through the Reaffirmation of the Baptismal Covenant. Yet these rituals presuppose much spiritual formation in order for those adults or parents of children who participate in them to understand them, and therefore, the educational programs of the church would need to focus much attention on the preparation of persons for baptism or baptismal renewal. Many churches are finding new excitement in their adult education and outreach programs as they have turned their church membership classes into more thorough preparation for Christian conversion, initiation and renewal.[14]

Another example of the holistic nature of liturgy is the connection of the Church Year to the process of Christian Initiation. As *The Book of Worship* reminds us, the season of Lent is the traditional period of preparation for persons who are going to be baptized.[15] The Easter Vigil (the first service of Easter), traditionally held late on Saturday evening, is the most significant day of the year for baptism. This year at Easter in our congregation, several adults and children were baptized (by immersion!) as the congregation gathered around them, joyfully commemorating Christ's resurrection.

The Christian Year, with its two foci in Easter and Christmas, centers the church's experience of time around the events of Jesus' life—his incarnation, suffering, death, resurrection, ascension, and sending of the Holy Spirit at Pentecost. The "time" aspect of liturgy is often overlooked, but we believe it to be an important aspect of a holistic understanding of worship. It provides a way for us to engage the stories of our own lives with the story of Jesus.

4. *Worship in the emerging church will center on the church's identity as the Body of Christ.* At the center of worship will be the church's weekly celebration of Word and Table. In the basic pattern of our ritual, in our Sunday worship we hear the word of God read from the Bible and preached from the pulpit. We offer our praise to God, and we pray for the state of the church and the world. We acknowledge our gratitude for all God gives to us through the Great Thanksgiving of the Lord's Supper. This prayer of thanksgiving connects us to the past and to the future, as we proclaim, "Christ has died, Christ is risen, Christ will come again." Through it we pray "that we may be the Body of Christ for the world, redeemed by his blood." While the Ritual allows for churches to abbreviate the

order of worship for those days when the Lord's Supper is not celebrated, the pattern presupposes that Word *and* Table is the regular order of worship. For the majority of United Methodist congregations, the celebration of the Lord's Supper probably feels like something has been added on to our standard, weekly preaching service. The United Methodist Ritual, on the other hand, presupposes that when the church does not go to the table, we have left something off. This is a major paradigm shift.

A United Methodist congregation in northern Indiana spent several years studying the history and meaning of the Lord's Supper before deciding as a congregation that they should begin to emulate the early church by having weekly Eucharist. After they discovered that Sunday was the one day when the city's soup kitchen was closed, the congregation began to offer an open fellowship meal to their poor, inner-city neighborhood. To provide this ministry, the congregation divided up into teams, and each week one of the teams provided a Sunday dinner after church for whoever wanted to come. Their rationale: we become the Body of Christ through the Lord's Supper; therefore we must continue Christ's table fellowship to include our whole neighborhood.[16] That is the central action of our worship: to make us into the Body of Christ for the world.

CONCLUSION

Our United Methodist Ritual connects us to the universal church, grounds us in a local congregation, offers us a holistic framework for ministry, and forms us as the Body of Christ in the world. It is just as accessible for large congregations as it is for the small, rural church (such as the ones we grew up attending). As a humanly produced document, our Ritual is certainly not perfect, and over time the Holy Spirit may help us to do even better. But, we certainly can do worse. Why should we settle for junk food when we can feast at a banquet? Our Ritual has the obvious potential to shape us into the Body of Christ as the emerging megachurch of the twenty-first century.

Nevertheless, it can *only* do this for us if we allow the Ritual to renew us, to challenge us, and to bless us through our active participation in worship. Our ritual is meant to be *done*, and it must be done well and with passion. We have a Roman Catholic friend who once said to us that no one should be allowed to be a priest until he has shown that he knows how to throw an excellent party. We believe this is true of all worship leaders. We absolutely *must* learn how to enable people to celebrate together as Body of Christ. All parties take good planning and gracious implementation. We have our plan in the Ritual—we can do no better. Let us *use* our Ritual and see what God will do through us in the new millennium as we await the fulfillment of God's New Creation.

ENDNOTES

[1] Eric Milner-White, *UMH* 335.

[2] "Alive and vital" is the favorite redundancy in church renewal literature.

[3] Revelation 21, selected verses.

[4] For background to this section, see Roy A Rappaport, *Ritual and Religion in the Making of Humanity* (Cambridge: Cambridge University Press, 1999) 23-68.

[5] For example, the Eastern Orthodox Churches' *Liturgy of St. John Chrysostom.*

[6] Our youngest daughter was baptized by immersion at two months of age. We would *love* to show you the photographs!

[7] Or, as Rappaport says, ritual is "self-referential" and "canonical."

[8] Compare Services I and IV in the hymnal to observe the different orientations.

[9] Under subsection, "The Gathered Community/ The Whole Assembly," page 20 in the pdf. edition.

[10] *UMH* 34.

[11] *The United Methodist Book of Worship* 446.

[12] Pentecostal or Charismatic churches practice a similar prayer form, though often the prayer will be in the form of glossolalia, "speaking in tongues."

[13] Thomas Ken, adapted by Gilbert H. Vieira, *UMH* 94.

[14] For an excellent United Methodist resource see Daniel T. Benedict, *Come to the Waters: Baptism and Our Ministry of Welcoming Seekers and Welcoming Disciples* (Nashville: Discipleship Resources, 1996).

[15] *The United Methodist Book of Worship,* 320.

[16] This church is Broadway Christian Parish United Methodist Church in South Bend, Indiana. In 2000 there were at least 15 United Methodist Churches in the United States that used the Word and Table pattern for their principal worship service each Sunday. Since the adoption of *This Holy Mystery* in 2004, that number is much larger, possibly in the hundreds, though at this writing we do not have accurate statistics

Select Bibliography

In this short bibliography, we provide material from a variety of perspectives, including some of those we critique in this book. We *do not* recommend all the positions represented below, some of which contradict our own proposals. We do, however, recommend that worship leaders try to understand the positions with which they *do not* agree.

Resources for worship committees and pastors:

Anderson, Byron, ed. *Worship Matters: A United Methodist Guide to Worship Work.* Vols. I & II. Nashville: Discipleship Resources, 1999.

Benedict, Daniel T. & Miller, Craig Kennet. *Contemporary Worship for the 21ˢᵗ Century.* Nashville: Discipleship Resources, 1998.

Bradshaw, Paul, ed. *The New Westminster Dictionary of Liturgy and Worship.* Louisville: Westminster/John Knox, 2002.

Felton, Gayle Carlton, *The Holy Myster: A United Methodist Understanding of Holy Communion.* Nashville: Discipleship Resources, 2005.

Langford, Andy. *Transitions in Worship.* Nashville: Abingdon Press, 1999.

Lathrop, Gordon. *What are the essentials of Christian worship?* Minneapolis: Augsburg Fortress Publishers, 1994.

Moeller, Pamela Ann. *Exploring Worship Anew.* St. Louis: Chalice Press, 1998.

Van Dyk, Leanne, ed. *A More Profound Alleluia: Theology and Worship in Harmony.* Grand Rapids, Eerdmans, 2005.

Webber, Robert. *Blended Worship: Achieving Substance and Relevance in Worship.* Peabody, Mass: Hendrickson, 1996.

————-*Planning Blended Worship.* Nashville: Abingdon, 1998.

————*Renew Your Worship: A Study in the Blending of Traditional and Contemporary Worship.* Peabody, MA: Hendrickson Publishers, 1997.

White, James. *Introduction to Christian Worship.* Third edition, revised. Nashville: Abingdon, 2000.

Preaching, media and liturgy resources:

Childers, Jana. *Performing the Word.* Nashville: Abingdon Press, 1998.

Imaging the Word: An Arts and Lectionary Resource. Edited by Susan Blain. Cleveland: United Church Press, 1996.

Killinger, John. *Preaching the New Millennium.* Nashville: Abingdon Press, 1999.

Troeger, Thomas H. *Preaching While the Church is Under Reconstruction: The Visionary Role of Preachers in a Fragmented World.* Nashville: Abingdon Press, 1999.

Discussion of the traditional and contemporary worship style:

Dawn, Marva J. *Reaching Out Without Dumbing Down: A Theology of Worship for the Turn-of-the-Century Culture.* Grand Rapids: Eerdmans, 1995.

Johnson, Todd E, ed. *The Conviction of Things Not Seen: Worship and Ministry in the 21st Century.* Grand Rapids: Brazos Press, 2002.

Westermeyer, Paul, Bosch, Paul and Sawicki, Marianne. *What is "contemporary" worship?* Minneapolis: Augsburg Fortress Publishers, 1995.

Wright, Tim. *A Community of Joy: How to Create Contemporary Worship.* Nashville: Abingdon Press, 1994.

Christian initiation and reaching out to "seekers":
Benedict, Dan. *Come To The Waters: Baptism and Our Ministry of Welcoming Seekers and Making Disciples.* Nashville: Discipleship Resources, 1996.
Easum, William. *How to Reach Baby Boomers.* Nashville: Abingdon Press, 1991.
Felton, Gayle Carlton. *By Water and the Spirit: Making Connections for Identity and Ministry.* Nashville: Discipleship Resources, 1997.
Scifres, Mary J. *Searching for Seekers: Ministry with a New Generation of the Unchurched.* Nashville: Abingdon Press, 1998.

Theology, worship and culture:
Clapp, Rodney. *A Peculiar People: The Church as Culture in a Post-Christian Society.*
Jennings, Jr., Theodore W. *Life As Worship: Prayer and Praise in Jesus' Name.* Grand Rapids: Wm. B. Eerdmans Publishing Co., 1982.
Redman, Robb. *The Great Worship Awakening: Singing a New Song in the Postmodern Church.* San Francisco: Jossey-Bass, 2002.
Saliers, Don E. *Worship Come to Its Senses.* Nashville: Abingdon Press, 1996.

Pastoral leadership:
Bandy, Thomas G. *Moving Off the Map.* Nashville: Abingdon Press, 1998.
Easum, William. *Dancing with Dinosaurs: Ministry in a Hostile and Hurting World.* Nashville: Abingdon Press, 1993.
Wills, Dick. *Waking to God's Dream.* Nashville: Abingdon Press, 1999.